Choosing a Dog

Choosing a Dog

A Guide to Picking the Perfect Breed

Nancy Baer
and Steve Duno

BERKLEY BOOKS, NEW YORK

Cover photograph courtesy of George Wirt, Bide-A-Wee Adoptions;
cover models courtesy of Bide-A-Wee Adoptions.

CHOOSING A DOG

A Berkley Book / published by arrangement with
the author

PRINTING HISTORY
Berkley trade paperback edition / December 1995

The Penguin Putnam Inc. World Wide Web site address is
http://www.penguinputnam.com

ISBN: 0-425-14958-7

BERKLEY®
Berkley Books are published by The Berkley Publishing Group,
a division of Penguin Putnam Inc.,
375 Hudson Street, New York, New York 10014.
BERKLEY and the "B" design
are trademarks belonging to Penguin Putnam Inc.

PRINTED IN THE UNITED STATES OF AMERICA

20   19   18   17   16   15   14   13   12

Contents

Section Four
The Working Group

Section Five
The Terrier Group

Section Six
The Toy Group

Section Seven
The Non-Sporting Group

Section Eight
The Herding Group

Section Nine
The Miscellaneous Group

Section Ten
Is There a Mutt in Your Life?

Section Eleven
Choosing the Right Dog from Within a Breed

Acknowledgments

We would like to thank our families and friends for their support during the making of this book. We would also like to thank our agent, Toni Lopopolo, for her friendship, patience and help in guiding us through the process for the first time. Thanks also goes out to our editor, Elizabeth Beier, as well as Jack and Colleen McDaniel and the entire staff at the Academy of Canine Behavior, without whose knowledge and expertise this book could not have been written. We are also grateful to Dr. Nanette Pasquini for supplying us with important canine medical information. Lastly, we would like to thank all of our dogs, especially Louie and Bliss.

Introduction

The Chihuahua and the Saint Bernard are, oddly enough, members of the same species, *Canis familiaris,* sharing the same genetic blueprint, anatomy, and fundamental drives. Over the years, however, humans have engineered amazing variations within this species, selectively breeding animals that exhibit physical and behavioral characteristics most suitable for a variety of needs such as herding, guarding, or running. The dog was and arguably still is the most manipulated animal on earth. Its historic role as worker and servant has now been largely replaced by one less utilitarian; today our dogs are for the most part companions.

What many potential dog owners fail to consider is that the unique physical and behavioral variations created over the years are still valid today. Though the Chihuahua and the Saint Bernard share basic drives, they are radically different both behaviorally and structurally. Chihuahuas are high-strung, delicate, long-lived yappers; Saint Bernards are lumbering, powerful, short-lived droolers. Which is more suited to apartment life? Which is more tolerant of children? Which will have fewer medical problems? Which is easier to housetrain?

Dog owners quickly run into problems when the breed-specific behavior of the dog they have chosen begins to clash with their lifestyle and personality. A herding breed, such as a Shetland Sheepdog, may not be the best choice for a family with young children, because a Sheltie may instinctively herd the children as if they were sheep, chasing them and perhaps even nipping at their heels. Shelties may also want to chase bikes, cars, and joggers, and they sometimes bark excessively. They are not necessarily being bad; they're just doing what they were bred to do. Training can modify

1

these types of behavior, but the instinct will always be there. That same family would do better with a Golden Retriever, a breed that normally loves children and will endure almost unlimited physical attention from them. Retrievers have a history of working closely with humans; the dog goes out into the water, picks up the duck, then immediately returns to the hunter. In comparison, a herding breed's task is more complex and may involve little human interaction for long periods. The herding dog's job requires more intelligence and a more independent mindset.

Those who buy a dog for purely aesthetic reasons may end up with a breed whose behavior clashes with their lifestyle. Problems ranging from property destruction to fear-biting to outright dominance aggression can result. By choosing the right breed you can avoid much heartache.

Each day at our training facility, we field calls from people wondering what breed would suit them. Though they have usually done some research, they are unfortunately at the mercy of highly subjective reading material, and more often than not have narrowed down their choices without considering their situation. Much of our business as trainers comes from the mismatch of dog to owner. We know firsthand that potential owners need to make more educated choices and to have a sourcebook they can trust.

This book is written from a trainer's standpoint and is designed to educate you about the breed-specific behavioral and structural characteristics of dogs. It will also discuss how to use this knowledge in choosing a dog to fit your personality and lifestyle.

We train hundreds of dogs each year and have come to understand the unique character of each breed. We do not have the bias or favoritism that breeders or breed aficionados possess. They love their respective breeds; the literature they generate does not always speak frankly about potential problems inherent in their breed. In this book we will give you an honest behavioral and structural profile of each AKC-registered breed as well as several breeds not currently recognized by the AKC. We will also tell you how responsive each breed is to training, and we'll discuss the environment and personality types that are suitable or unsuitable for each. In addition, we will discuss mixed breeds and hybrids, breeders, how to pick the right individual dog once the breed is chosen, and how to adopt a dog.

How Not to Buy a Dog

Many people use a questionable decision-making process in picking a dog. Some choose a dog the way they would a piece of furniture. Is it pretty? Is it too large for the apartment? Some choose a dog as if it were a firearm. How powerful is it? Will it be an efficient deterrent to criminals? Does it look intimidating? Others choose out of pity. You mean you have to put those puppies to sleep? This old dog is lost and skinny as a rail. Daddy, if we don't keep her, I'll just die. . . .

Let's take a look at two classic examples of how not to choose a dog:

Scenario One

Saturday afternoon. Mrs. Plotkin is being walked through the mall by her two children, Maybelle and Otto, nine and seven years old. Maybelle is darting in and out of stores. Otto is thinking about crying. Mrs. Plotkin pleads with her daughter to put back the stuffed panther she has taken from a toy store. The saleswoman from the store comes out and takes back the panther. Maybelle gives her a dirty look, then runs over to her mother, crying. Otto joins in. At that moment Maybelle looks across the corridor at the display window of Bozo's Pet-O-Rama, and screams out, *"Puppies!"* She runs over and gawks at the puppies cavorting in their own little pens. Otto follows. There are four puppies: a Cocker Spaniel, an Akita, a Golden Retriever, and a Chinese Shar-Pei, all three to four months old. Mrs. Plotkin walks over slowly.

"I like the wrinkly one, Mommy!" says Maybelle.

The young sales clerk comes over; she is wearing a clean white smock with the name Julie stenciled on it. She is all smiles.

"What kind of dog is that?" asks Mrs. Plotkin.

"It's a Chinese Shar-Pei," says Julie, her arm around Maybelle. "Want to hold him?" she asks the girl.

"Yes! Yes!"

They all go inside the store. The clerk pulls the squirming puppy out of his pen and places him in front of Maybelle, who is sitting on the floor with Otto.

"Is it supposed to chew on their shoes like that?" asks Mrs. Plotkin.

"Oh, sure," says Julie, with reassuring authority. "That's what puppies do."

"He looks like a frog," says Otto, pulling on the puppy's tail.

"He is sort of cute," says Mrs. Plotkin, watching Maybelle's fascination with the dog.

"Let's get it, Mommy," screams Maybelle, as the puppy growls softly at Otto.

"I think we should call Daddy first."

"No! I want it! Now!" Maybelle screams. Otto looks at her in awe while the puppy chews on his shoelaces. Suddenly he starts bawling.

Mrs. Plotkin looks helplessly at Julie. "How much?"

Scenario Two

Three A.M. Jethro is working the graveyard shift at Mel's Gas 'n' Go in a dangerous part of town. A 1963 Chevy station wagon smokes up to the pumps. The driver gets out and limps over to the office.

Jethro, the station attendant, cautiously steps out. "Help you?"

"I'll trade you a puppy for a tank a gas," the driver says. "Come on over and check it out."

They walk over to the station wagon. A hand-painted sign on the side of the car reads: "Rottweiler pups, $50 or best offer." The driver lowers the tailgate; the smell of urine and feces wafts out. Six puppies are in the back, some asleep, some wandering about.

"Their father was a champion," says the man, grabbing the largest puppy by the scruff of the neck and handing it to Jethro. The puppy howls.

"This one's the best. It's got spirit."

"It's scared of me."

"That's 'cause you're a stranger to him. He's only four weeks old, you know."

Jethro holds the screaming dog tightly. "He's peeing on me."

"He's just a puppy. So what do you say? This dog will protect you real good."

"How big will he get?"

"As big as you."

"Yeah?"

"Oh, yeah."

"I got kids. Will he like kids?"

"Oh, heck, this breed just loves kids. You'll see. He won't let anyone near your kids. . . . So what do you say?"

"Well, go on, fill 'er up."

Think these scenarios aren't played out every day? Think again. Most people don't have a clue to what they are getting into when they choose a dog. They pick a breed purely for aesthetic reasons, for protection, out of a misguided notion of machismo, or under pressure from their kids. An elderly widow buys a Bullmastiff because she is afraid to live alone. A young couple running a day-care business out of their house adopt a nine-month-old unneutered male Akita as a playmate for the kids. These people could have major problems sooner or later because the breed they have picked in no way matches their lifestyle, personality, or environment. They will end up hiring trainers to solve problems that might have been avoided by making a careful decision based not on impulse and emotion but on family dynamics, need, environment, and the personalities of the owners. If the Plotkins went shopping for a car, would they come home with a two-seater sports car or a minivan? Would they let their kids decide?

As trainers and behaviorists, we have seen the same scenario played out again and again: the wrong dog in the wrong hands spells trouble. What kind of trouble? It varies. The worst-case scenario is of course an attack by a dog on a human, which is an all too common occurrence these days. More than a million dog bites were reported in this country last year. We have all heard the chilling stories of a child being mauled by a Rottweiler, a Pit Bull, or a dog of some other formidable breed. Did you know, however, that Cocker Spaniels and Dalmatians lead the list of breeds most likely to bite? Size does not necessarily equate to the potential for aggression.

What other problems can occur? Destructive behavior, barking, car-chasing, running away, medical problems—the list goes on. Though much undesirable behavior in dogs does stem from inappropriate or nonexistent training or from an unfavorable environment, some of it is hereditary or breed-specific.

Let's return to our scenarios. First, the Plotkins. Mom has no control over her own pack, let alone a Shar-Pei puppy. She is not thinking about that, though; she is thinking that a puppy might be a great distraction for her little tyrants, a great way to keep them occupied and out of her hair. Bozo's Pet-O-Rama strikes again. Located in a busy suburban mall, the store places puppies of various aesthetically interesting breeds in the window to seduce the Plotkins of the world. And it works. Pet shops do major business in this country selling poor-quality puppies of all shapes and sizes, most or all of them acquired from puppy mills in the Midwest, which churn out hundreds of substandard dogs year after year to satisfy demand. (We will discuss pet stores at greater length in the book.)

Let's look at the puppies available at Bozo's Pet-O-Rama. First, most of them are four months old—*red flag*. Why were these dogs not purchased when they were eight to ten weeks old? Second, look at the breeds. One of the dogs in the store window is an Akita, a beautiful, full-coated breed with a panda bear look to it. Kids love the look, but Akitas can be quite dominant, and they don't always interact well with young children. They need strong leadership.

The Pet-O-Rama is also offering a Cocker Spaniel, one of America's favorite breeds. In our experience, however, Cockers are often quite wary of children, and they are resistant to obedience training. Of all the breeds we work with, this one tops the list of dogs most likely to bite.

Next is the Golden Retriever, a good family breed that is tolerant of kids, very forgiving and eager to please. Not the brightest breed, but very trainable. From a reputable breeder, this dog would not be a bad choice, even for a family like the Plotkins.

Bozo, however, sharp businessman that he is, also has a Chinese Shar-Pei puppy in the window. Shar-Peis are expensive, and they're strangely adorable as puppies, with plenty of wrinkles and folds of skin. They are unusual enough in appearance to attract customers' attention, so the Plotkins are a perfect mark for this one. Unfortunately, the Shar-Pei is probably the last breed this family should consider. Many of them are aloof and extremely dominant; they do not like excessive handling and are very resistant to even the most fundamental training.

Jethro, the gas station attendant, works two jobs. He was robbed at gunpoint a few months before. He thinks a big dog might be a good insurance policy. Enter the 1963 Chevy filled with Rottweiler pups—the last breed to be careless with. Poor Jethro. We all know the stories of the vicious canine killers. This is a breed that inspires fear and respect in even the most cavalier passerby. When acquired through a diligent breeder and trained early on, Rottweilers can be affectionate, loyal pets. Make no mistake, though; you will need to prove your leadership every day with a Rottweiler, even under ideal circumstances. Jethro's situation couldn't be worse—breeder from hell, questionable lineage and health, no parents to observe, and puppies far too young to leave the litter. Jethro is headed for disaster. Better to be robbed at gunpoint.

Why Are the Breeds So Different?

In the Introduction, we discussed just how diversified the species *Canis familiaris* has become as a result of the selective breeding efforts of humankind. Why was this done?

Dogs are smart creatures, and so are humans. Humans recognized long ago the potential benefit of establishing a partnership with dogs. Dogs are easy to train because they are loyal to their leadership hierarchy. Once a leader is identified, the other members of the pack will do just about anything to support that leader. This is the reason that dogs are easier to train than cats; it's not that they are smarter, it's just that they have an instinctual allegiance to the pack and the pack leader. Cats—except for lions and, to a lesser extent, cheetahs—are not pack animals and do not have a well-defined group mentality.

Early human hunter-gatherers realized that the canine pack leader could be replaced by a human. The survival of the human tribe at that time depended in part on the success of the hunt. We humans, however, have never been the physical equal of our prey; we are slow, low on endurance, and sensorially inept in comparison to animals. The only advantages we had were our intellect, our tribal loyalty, and, like the dog, our ability to work cohesively as a team.

Our chief competitors at the time included the canids, or wild dogs, some of which hunted in well-choreographed packs. Dogs could run faster and longer than humans. They could operate masterfully as a team and pick up a scent where no scent was discernible to humans. By establishing a partnership with canids, we could greatly increase our chances of a productive hunt. But which species would be the best candidate for domestication? The fox, a solitary nocturnal creature, has no pack order at all; no pecking order is established in the litter, and except during mating, the fox exhibits no social organization. Coyotes and certain types of jackals form permanent male-female pair-bonds, but they do not establish permanent pack associations. Wolves, African hunting dogs, and dingoes all have a well-defined pack hierarchy in place, and all exhibit complex social interaction. Because these two ingredients seem to help create greater cognitive ability, these animals were the most likely candidates for domestication.

Domestication required more than simply changing behavior patterns, however; the animal itself had to be physically changed through selective breeding to better suit our needs. Wild wolf bitches come into season only once a year, in harmony with their prey's season. Domestic dog bitches come into heat two to three times a year; this allows for more rapid selective breeding to occur. Also, most wild dogs do not reach sexual maturity until they are two years of age, whereas domestic dogs are sexually capable at six to nine months. Also, male wolves are potent only during the breeding season, whereas male domestic dogs are always potent. An additional change was selectively bred into domesticated dogs: the elimination of monogamy, which would have seriously slowed down the selective breeding process. These new traits that were bred into the domestic dog can be maintained only under domesticity; they would cause insurmountable social problems in the wild.

The perfect symbiotic relationship was born: dogs would aid us in the hunt in exchange for access to safe shelter, a reliable food supply, and protection from predators. A by-product of this for both parties was companionship, a camaraderie that both species thrived on.

With the advent of herding, humankind again called upon the assistance of the dog. Some nomadic tribes found it easier to domesticate and maintain a steady stock of animals year-round than to depend on the fortunes of the hunt. This pastoral way of life created a more stable supply of food and clothing, encouraged the establishment of semipermanent villages, and allowed for the development of elementary economic and political systems. Early Semitic tribes in Mesopotamia used breeds similar to the present-day Kuvasz, a large, powerful white herd-guarding dog that often prefers the company of sheep to that of people. Dogs were now needed not to kill prey but to keep herds of sheep, goats, reindeer, or cattle together; to move the herds from place to place; and to protect them from predators and poachers.

The diversity of dog breeds increased in direct proportion to the jobs they needed to fill. One of the earliest breeds to be developed for a specific task was the sight hound. Greyhound- and Wolfhound-type dogs were bred and highly prized by Egyptian and Assyrian nobility as far back as 5000 years ago. Hunting dogs in desert lands depended less on their noses, given the sandy soil's inability to hold scent for very long. In addition, the topography was one of rolling plains and open country; prey was easily visible to dogs with good eyesight. The arid, wide-open expanses also required these dogs to be fast, lightly built, and short-coated so as not to overheat the animal. They were perfectly suited to their task.

Heavier, mastiff-type breeds were first developed 3000 to 4000 years ago in Asia Minor (present-day Turkey) and gradually exported to Egypt, Assyria, Greece, and Italy. These powerful dogs were first used to take down large game; they would grab the prey's muzzle and hold on until the hunter arrived to make the kill. Rhodesian Ridgebacks were used by the Egyptians to flush lions for archers who were lying in wait. The Saluki, one of today's beautiful silky-haired sight hounds, was used thousands of years ago by Egyptian and Assyrian hunters as a coursing hound, to run down and capture rabbits and small gazelles. Salukis were so prized by their owners that they were carried from place to place by camels, so as not to burn their feet on the hot sand.

The hounds, the herders, and the mastiffs were the three main groups that had begun to emerge by Greco-Roman times. Odysseus, in Homer's epic *The Odyssey*, speaks of his faithful hound Argos, who when young was able to hunt deer and rabbit by scent or sight. The Rottweiler, a mastiff type, was used by Roman legions to herd and guard large flocks of sheep and cattle that were taken on the march to feed the troops.

By medieval times, Germanic tribes had developed scent hounds, dogs that located prey primarily by scent rather than sight. The thick forests of Europe did not offer clear sight lines to spot prey; Bloodhound- and Harrier-type dogs did better here. Once these dogs pick up a scent, they think of little else but finding its source. These same northern Europeans were also responsible for perfecting the flushing breeds, initially Poodle-type and then spaniel-type dogs that would flush game birds from cover, allowing trained falcons to intercept them in mid-flight. These same people also developed small courageous hunting dogs with great drive and stamina to find and kill beavers, badgers, and rats. Today these dogs make up the Terrier Group.

For most of history, dogs played a primarily utilitarian role, earning their keep and their owners' companionship only as a reward for a job well done. The notion of having a dog solely as a companion is a fairly recent development, though members of the ancient Egyptian, Greek, and Roman nobility did have companion lapdogs, notably the Maltese. Only in the nineteenth century did the perception of dogs merely as workers begin to shift in favor of simple companionship. The characteristic behavior of breeds created over the years has not changed, however. Today's Collies, for example, still have their herding instincts intact, even though most of them will never see a sheep.

The American Kennel Club currently lists 145 breeds. These breeds are divided into seven groups, plus one Miscellaneous Class, which includes breeds that are awaiting AKC approval and possible entry into one of the seven recognized groups. The seven groups are: Sporting, Hound, Working, Terrier, Toy, Non-Sporting, and Herding. Non-Sporting is a catch-all group for breeds that no longer have clearly defined roles, but each of the other groups has a unique, easily identifiable behavioral profile. We will go over these profiles in more detail in the following chapters.

Later in the book we will discuss mixed breeds, which are not recognized by the AKC but are certainly admired by us and by millions of others. We will also discuss hybrids.

The personality of a potential owner is one of the key ingredients that should be considered in the decision-making process. At our training facility, we work as much with the owners as with the dogs; we have found their temperaments to be as varied as those of the dogs. This can lead to problems if the owner's temperament clashes with that of the dog's. For example, some breeds absorb training at a slower rate and respond only to a patient, empathetic approach. An owner who is used to training Rottweilers, which need a more demanding training technique, will fail miserably if he or she uses the same assertive approach with a Belgian Sheepdog, a breed with a more delicate constitution. A Belgian needs an owner with patience and a keen awareness of the dog's state of mind. A high-strung or overbearing owner who lacks patience and foresight should avoid Belgians. Likewise, a mild, introverted, placating person will be overwhelmed by dominant breeds such as Rottweilers, German Shepherds, Akitas, or Chesapeake Bay Retrievers. A large, loud, physically imposing ex–football player should not pick an extremely submissive Italian Greyhound as his pet. The dog could be too intimidated to do anything but urinate submissively and shake. That same person would be better off with a fairly dominant male German Shepherd, a dog capable of appreciating a more imposing leader.

Honestly determine what your presentation to the dog will be like, both temperamentally and physically. Are you tall, short, mild-mannered, overly nurturing, loud, meek, impatient? Making an honest assessment of yourself now will aid you greatly when you go through the breed-specific profiles that follow.

Before we move on to Section Two, The Sporting Group, we would like to show you just how different breeds can be. Let's pick two breeds and compare and contrast them in terms of breed-specific behavior and physical characteristics. How about a German Shepherd and a Saluki?

Saluki	German Shepherd
sighthound	herding dog
average intelligence	highly intelligent
ancient breed	fairly new breed
lean, supple build	strongly built
short, silky coat	medium-length coat with shedding undercoat
40–60 pounds	60–100 pounds
excellent vision	average vision
average sense of smell	excellent sense of smell
no major health problems	prone to structural defects
not overly affectionate	very affectionate
aloof with strangers	suspicious of strangers
relatively quiet	can be a barker
not fond of children	good with family's children
not overly territorial	very territorial

Based on the information above, what type of environment do you feel each dog would do best in? Worst in? What type of owner would best suit each?

The behavioral and physiological information provided in Sections Two through Nine is statistically accurate. However, there are always exceptions. If improperly bred, trained, or handled, any breed can be aggressive. Likewise, if properly bred and expertly trained, even an inherently aggressive breed can be friendly and wonderful. These breed profiles are meant simply to supply the reader with benchmark information.

The Sporting Group

Pointers, setters, spaniels, and retrievers were originally bred to assist the hunter in finding, flushing, and retrieving game, usually birds, either on land or in water. Some breeds in this group, notably the pointers, remain primarily hunting dogs, whereas others, such as the Labrador Retriever, have been more successful in making the transition to house pet. Sporting dogs have great energy, stamina, and determination. Few of them would do well in an apartment. Their energy level requires owners to provide them with regular exercise and, ideally, with some type of job toward which to direct their energy. Their excellent sense of smell is a distraction to them, and can make obedience training difficult. Hunting is the most natural job for them, but fieldwork in water or land retrieving can work just as well. Dogs from this group should be owned by active persons who enjoy a busy dog. None of these breeds will be easygoing couch potatoes.

Brittany

Origins: First developed in eighteenth-century France, the Brittany is the archetype for bird dogs. It is valued for its sense of smell and its desire to work close to the hunter, a valuable asset in smaller suburban hunting arenas.

Appearance: The Brittany is a medium-size dog, standing approximately 17.5 to 20.5 inches at the shoulder and weighing 30 to 40 pounds. The legs are long in proportion to the body, giving the dog a lanky, squared-off appearance. The Brittany has an easily maintained coat that is shed seasonally and requires only periodic brushing and trimming. The color is white with liver or orange patches. The tail is docked.

Breed Profile: Brittany's are excellent bird dogs. Their smaller size allows them to go where larger breeds cannot. They are friendly, sensitive, intelligent dogs that are relatively easily to train. They are also very active, and need to have their enthusiasm channeled into some regular activity, such as hunting. Many owners acquire them primarily for hunting and are pleasantly surprised to find that their sweet disposition and desire to please makes them excellent family pets as well. They do well with children and other dogs.

Without exercise, however, they may begin to exhibit hyperactive, nervous tendencies. In lieu of hunting, an owner could help a Brittany release energy through retrieve or recall games, tricks and agility work, or some other form of directed exercise.

Overall, this is a fine family pet with few tendencies toward aggressive behavior. The few examples of aggression we have seen in Brittanys have been fear-based; they are sensitive dogs that do not respond well to heavy-handed training techniques or unfair treatment of any kind. The key to successfully owning this breed is fair, consistent training combined with socialization and some regular outdoor activity.

Best Home: A Brittany needs a house with a fenced yard, plenty of daily exercise, and early obedience training to contain and direct its enthusiasm. Hunting is a natural outlet for Brittanys. They are fine with children, as long as no roughhousing goes on. A Brittany owner should be an active person who prefers a high-energy dog to one that is easygoing. A nervous person who prefers personal space should avoid this breed. Elderly or disabled owners are fine provided they can exercise and train the dog efficiently.

Pointer

Origins: The Pointer is a specialist, bred for a specific purpose. First developed in northern Europe and Spain in the sixteenth century, this breed came into its own with the application of firearms for bird hunting, somewhere around the eighteenth century. Pointers are fine hunters; it is thrilling to see them go on  point upon locating a covey of birds. Even young pointer pups will point when they sense prey; pointing is instinctive rather than learned. These are hunting dogs, bred to a narrow purpose.

Appearance: Pointers stand approximately 24 to 28 inches at the shoulder and weigh between 50 and 70 pounds. They are very high energy dogs, with a lean, muscular build and a low-maintenance short, shedding coat. Because of this short coat, they don't fare well when left outside in cold climates. The color may be white with liver patches, solid black, or solid liver.

Breed Profile: Pointers are bred to have great stamina and to focus on their task with the determination of a scent hound. When they pick up a scent, they will completely ignore you. Forget about getting them to come to you until they have completed their mission. They are not extremely bright, but they are driven.

Because of their energy and their slim, muscular build, Pointers can make great jogging partners. They are usually friendly with strangers and quite tolerant of children, although in their excitement to play they can knock small children down. They also get along quite well with other dogs.

Pointers don't make great house pets. It's like having a Ferrari in your kitchen. Their constant frenetic pace can be quite draining to the owner who attempts to share the house with one. Obedience training helps tremendously, but again, why choose a breed that, by design, is meant for a very specific purpose, one that is far from the congenial house pet most of us desire?

Best Home: Pointers need to direct their energy into some task. Hunting is the most natural choice. If you choose a Pointer, we recommend that you use the dog for hunting on a regular basis. These dogs certainly do not belong in an apartment in the city; they require a fenced yard or kennel.

The owner of a Pointer must be able to tolerate the dog's high-strung, task-oriented temperament. This will not be a lazy, foot-warming pet. If you like your space, avoid this breed.

Joggers can do well with a Pointer; the dog's trim, athletic physique make it a perfect running companion, and the exercise will help calm the Pointer down.

Don't leave a Pointer alone for too long. It is likely to become noisy and destructive.

We advise the elderly and the disabled to avoid this breed. Pointers are just too frenetic. Children are okay, as long as playtime does not get too rough. These dogs can knock a small child down and cause injury.

Early obedience training is a must. The owner must have time available for this.

Pointer, German Shorthaired

Origins: First established in eighteenth- and nineteenth-century Germany, the German Shorthaired Pointer was developed by crossing the Pointer with German foxhound types. It has greater scenting ability than the Pointer, is less averse to water, has greater stamina, and is thus a more versatile hunting dog.

Appearance: The German Shorthaired Pointer stands 21 to 25 inches at the shoulder, and weighs 45 to 70 pounds. The shedding coat is short and easy to maintain, requiring only periodic brushing. The color is liver with small white markings.

Breed Profile: Like all hunting dogs, this breed is extremely active, perhaps even more so than the Pointer. It will be more distractable as well, due to its superior scent ability. German Shorthaired Pointers are stubborn much to the dismay of the unsuspecting owner looking for an easygoing house pet. This dog is designed to do a specific task, namely to hunt. Any owner who does not give this breed regular tasks such as hunting or tracking may soon be living with a dog that is vocal, destructive, neurotic, and hyperactive.

German Shorthaired Pointers get along well with children and other dogs. They also tend to accept strangers after an initial introductory period.

Best Home: This is not a breed that will curl up in front of the fireplace all day. These dogs need structured activity, the kind that a hunter would provide. A house with a fenced yard is mandatory. Their level of activity is intense and can be stressful to easygoing persons. Patience and firm leadership are essential, as is early obedience training, especially the Come command, which may be difficult to teach because of this breed's scenting ability. Without a job to do, this breed will drive you up the wall. Joggers do well with this breed. The elderly or disabled may have trouble controlling this active breed.

Pointer, German Wirehaired

Origins: Developed in the late nineteenth century in Germany, this breed retained the versatility of the German Shorthaired Pointer, but added the all-weather protection of a coarse, wiry coat, allowing it to deal with rougher hunting conditions and colder weather.

Appearance: The German Wirehaired Pointer stands approximately 22 to 26 inches at the shoulder and weighs 50 to 70 pounds. It has a strong, well-muscled body. Its medium-maintainance shedding coat is of medium length, coarse and wiry, and water resistant. The coat color is liver-and-white. The thin undercoat sheds out during the summer. Periodic brushing will help prevent matting.

Breed Profile: This is another all-purpose hunting dog and is therefore not very adaptable to quiet family living. These are high-energy dogs that need lots of exercise. They are more aloof and independent than the other pointers, exhibiting an almost terrier-

like temperament. They can be quite stubborn and are usually suspicious of strangers. We do not recommend them for families with
young children. This breed needs early obedience training as well
as early socialization with people and other dogs. These dogs may
become destructive if bored or left isolated; they also bark quite a
lot. The German Wirehaired Pointer's scenting ability will work
against you during obedience training particularly when you're
teaching the Come command. Once these pointers pick up a scent,
they will ignore you completely, but this is what they are bred to
do. They are not bred to be quiet, easygoing family dogs.

Best Home: A house with a fenced yard is essential. A hunter would
best be able to provide this breed with purpose and a proper level
of activity. The owner should by all means have good leadership
skills and ample time to provide the dog with basic obedience training and socialization. We do not recommend this breed for those
with young children. Also, those who are unable to deal with a busy,
high-energy dog should not consider this breed. An owner who jogs
might find this breed to be an excellent running partner because
of its lithe, muscular body.

Retriever, Chesapeake Bay

Origins: Perfected in nineteenth-century Maryland, this
breed filled the need for a dog
that could retrieve ducks all
day in the cold, turbulent wa-
ters of the Chesapeake Bay. Its
greater size and strength gave
it an edge over the Labrador
Retriever.

Appearance: The Chesapeake
Bay Retriever stands approximately 21 to 26 inches at the shoulder

and weighs 60 to 90 pounds. It has a powerful medium- to large-boned structure. Its shedding, water-resistant wavy coat, which is relatively short and easy to maintain, does an excellent job of insulating the dog against cold water. A twice-weekly brushing should keep the coat in good condition. The color may be brown or tan.

Breed Profile: This is a big, strong dog with great courage and stamina. Chessies are hardy and impervious to inclement weather. They truly love the water. They are also extremely dominant, obstinate dogs that require strong, no-nonsense leadership. Without it, they will walk all over you. They are very stubborn and territorial and can be quite dog-aggressive, much more so than a Lab. We do not recommend Chesapeakes for families with young children because of their physical, controlling demeanor. They are not beyond snapping at a member of the family whom they regard as their subordinate, if they feel it is necessary from a disciplinary standpoint. They are very suspicious of strangers and are excellent watchdogs. The owner of a Chessie should start obedience training and socialization as early as possible. Those who wish to avoid some of the breed's inherent dominant aggressive behavior would do well to select a female. Some Chessies suffer from hip dysplasia and bloat, a life-threatening gaseous swelling and twisting of the stomach that may be caused by the consumption of too large a meal. We recommend feeding any large breed twice a day instead of once, to cut down on the volume of food in the stomach at any given time.

Best Home: The owner of a Chessie must be a strong, consistent leader right from the start. These dogs will quickly fill any leadership vacuum, and a spoiling, nurturing owner may be overwhelmed by the time the dog is six months old.

This is not a dog for the elderly or the disabled. Chessies quickly perceive physical weakness or lack of confidence in an owner and will soon take over.

A house with a fenced yard is mandatory. If left alone too long, this breed may bark excessively and be very destructive.

Obedience training and socialization with people and dogs

should start from day one. If you want a good watchdog that will be affectionate, intelligent, and athletic, and if you have great leadership skills and time to socialize the dog, then you may wish to consider a Chessie.

Retriever, Curly-Coated

Origins: Considered the oldest of the retrievers, the Curly-Coated Retriever traces its origins back to sixteenth-century England, perhaps a result of the mixing of Irish Water Spaniel, Poodle, and setter bloodlines. The outcome was a dog that would eagerly retrieve waterfowl from lakes or bays without being affected by the cold, thanks to its water-resistant coat.

Appearance: The Curly-Coated Retriever stands approximately 22 to 25 inches at the shoulder and weighs between 55 and 75 pounds. It has a strong medium-size body. The weather-resistant shedding coat is tightly curled and needs to be brushed several times a week. The coat may be black or liver-colored.

Breed Profile: This breed is affectionate but less eager to please than the Labrador Retriever. Curly-Coated Retrievers are also slightly less active, more independent, more stubborn, and not as likely to welcome strangers. They can make good family pets, but they need more socialization than a Lab, and they will not tolerate rough-housing from children the way a Lab would. They need regular exercise. Curly-Coated Retrievers need obedience training early on, but they require a more patient training technique than a Lab. They are more sensitive and will shut down on you if you are not slow and consistent with your technique.

Best Home: A house with a fenced yard is essential. Children are okay, but no roughhousing should be tolerated. Socialization with people and dogs should begin early, as should obedience training. A firm yet patient leader is called for with this breed. The elderly and the disabled should consider another breed. Cautious or nervous persons should not consider this breed, nor should those who do not have time to work the dog. A hunter would find this breed to be an excellent water retriever.

Retriever, Flat-Coated

Origins: The Flat-Coated Retriever originated in early nineteenth-century England and was the preferred retriever before the introduction of the Labrador. The breed was probably the result of mixing Newfoundland, setter, and spaniel bloodlines. It filled the need for a versatile hunter-retriever in water or on land.

Appearance: The Flat-Coated Retriever stands approximately 22 to 24.5 inches at the shoulder and weighs 60 to 80 pounds. The medium-length shedding coat is straight and needs to be brushed two or three times a week. The color may be black or liver.

Breed Profile: The Flat-Coated Retriever has not been commercialized to the same extent that the Labrador Retriever has been. Its temperament is somewhere in between that of the Curly-Coated and the Labrador. It is not quite reserved, but not as gregarious and accepting of strangers as a Golden or Lab. This makes it a better watchdog than the Lab. It is slightly less energetic than a Lab, and more sensitive. Because of this, you cannot use quite the same degree of firmness in training that you might use with the more gregarious Lab.

We have found these dogs to be more prone to fear-based aggression than Labs or Goldens, and they need early socialization with people and dogs to help counteract this. They are normally good with the children in their own family, but they may show initial suspicion toward the children's friends. Do not let your children roughhouse with this breed the way they might with a Lab or a Golden. These dogs have a great nose, which can lead them astray sometimes, so early obedience training is a must. As with any medium to large dog, this breed can be succeptible to hip dysplasia and bloat.

Best Home: This breed needs a house with a fenced yard. Apartments are not a good idea. The owner of a Flat-Coated Retriever must be a patient, consistent leader and must desire an active dog. Time to exercise the dog must be available every day. A hunter would do well with this breed. Obedience training and socialization should begin early and continue throughout the dog's life. This is an active breed that may not suit an elderly or disabled person. As with any breed that shows suspicion of strangers, it is important for the owner to be confident and calm rather than cautious around new people, dogs, and circumstances.

Retriever, Golden

Origins: Developed in mid-nineteenth-century England, the Golden Retriever is a versatile retriever in or out of water. Water Spaniel, Newfoundland, and Irish Setter bloodlines were used to arrive at today's dog.

Appearance: The Golden Retriever stands approximately 22 to 24.5 inches at the shoulder and weighs between 55 and 80 pounds. It has a strong, robust, athletic body. Its reddish to blond shedding coat is of medium length and requires a good brushing at least every other day. The color ranges from red to tan to light blond.

Breed Profile: Few breeds are as endearing, playful, and eager to please as the Golden Retriever. Despite the breed's great popularity, the quality of breeding has remained fairly constant, with some minor exceptions.

The Golden Retriever has become perhaps as versatile as the German Shepherd. Goldens are used as hunters, as competition obedience dogs, as guide and service dogs, as search-and-rescue dogs, and as film and television stars. Their versatility comes not from their level of intelligence, which is average at best, but from their great devotion to humans, a trait common to most retrievers.

Goldens are athletic dogs and need regular exercise. They make excellent family pets and are capable of taking endless attention from children. They love it. They think it's fun to have a three-year-old on their back and a four-year-old tugging on their ears. Don't try that with a Rottweiler. Goldens are also quite accepting of strangers, quickly warming up to anyone or any dog. Because of this, they don't always make good guard dogs. They may lick a burglar to death. A Golden will wander off with anyone, so keep your eye on it. They aren't the most loyal dogs, because of their happy, sociable nature.

We recommend that you get a Golden Retriever bred for show and not for field work, unless you intend to hunt with the dog on a regular basis. A field-bred dog will be filled with nervous energy and will drive you nuts.

A few problems may arise with this breed. First, they can be overly playful and will constantly desire your attention and love. This can be persistent and annoying. If you sometimes wants your space, then get a Saluki, not a Golden Retriever. Obedience training is crucial for Goldens; their goofy, playful mind-set can get annoying after a while, so it's important to teach them to think instead of just react.

Second, we have recently seen some aggressive Goldens, most of them with the reddish coat. It is sad and sobering to see this behavior in such a happy, sociable breed. This is an unpredictable type of aggression that appears to be hereditary rather than learned. Sadly, once a Golden becomes aggressive, it is nearly impossible to turn the dog around. Some of these aggressive dogs have a hypoactive thyroid condition, which may be a contributing factor. We believe the root of the problem to be inconsistent, careless breeding. When breeders value looks over temperament, they open up Pandora's box. Get a Golden from a responsible breeder who breeds for temperament first, and make sure you see the parents and the rest of the litter. And please stay away from pet shops!

Best Home: A house with a fenced yard is essential. Goldens are active dogs that don't do well in an apartment. They usually do very well with children, and are normally friendly to everyone. They can be pushy with their affection, so the owner of a Golden must start obedience training early on and must not spoil the dog. Goldens are not the best guard dogs, so if that's a concern, consider another breed, perhaps a Flat-Coated Retriever. They are very active dogs, and may not be the best choice for the elderly or disabled.

Retriever, Labrador

Origins: The Labrador Retriever originated not in Labrador, but in Newfoundland and was perfected in England in the nineteenth century as a versatile land and water retriever with good scenting ability.

Appearance: The Labrador Retriever stands 21 to 24.5 inches at the shoulder, though there are some bred slightly shorter, and weighs between 50 and 80 pounds. It has a strong, muscular, sturdy body of medium size and a short, smooth, water-resistant shedding coat that is very easy to care for. The color may be black, chocolate, or yellow. The Labrador Retriever has webbed feet to aid in swimming.

Breed Profile: Labs are athletic, active dogs with boundless stamina and energy. They are natural retrievers and can't get enough of the water. Their immense popularity has created a field-versus-show schism in breed types, the field-bred Labs being much more energetic than the show dogs. These field-bred Labs do not make good house pets; you would be better off going to a breeder who produces show lines and can provide you with a much calmer, more thoughtful pet.

Labs are gregarious and often show great affection for children, adults, and even strangers. Because of this, they may not be extremely loyal; they may go off with anyone who flashes a smile. They have a "love me, touch me" attitude and thrive on human contact. This can be tiresome for those who are not used to the retriever mentality. Labs may try to control you with affection and with their high level of activity; the challenge in training them is to direct their energy into positive activity.

Though better than Golden Retrievers at watching the house, Labs are still not the best at this, certainly not as good as a German Shepherd or a Mastiff.

We have recently found slight variations in temperament among the three color variations. The blacks seem to be the most active and need the most exercise. The yellows tend to be the least thoughtful and confident and may show the most aggression. The chocolates, in our opinion, tend to be calmer and more thoughtful.

Though cases of aggression are rare, when a Lab does become aggressive it tends to be nearly impossible to turn around.

Best Home: A house with a fenced yard is essential. The ideal Lab owner is an active, sociable person who likes plenty of interaction with the dog. Don't get a Lab if you like space and need plenty of time to yourself. You won't get it with a Lab. Early obedience training is essential with such an energetic, athletic dog. The elderly and disabled may have trouble with this active breed.

Setter, English

Origins: First seen in sixteenth-century England, the English Setter was perfected as a hunting dog in the nineteenth century. In function they are almost identical to the Pointer. The major difference is the longer coat, which allows them to hunt in colder weather and gives them added protection against heavy undergrowth.

Appearance: The English Setter stands 22 to 25 inches at the shoulder and weighs between 50 and 70 pounds. The shedding coat is of medium length, flat and slightly wavy, and needs to be brushed frequently. The background color is normally white, with intermingled black, lemon, tan, or liver spotting.

Breed Profile: English Setters are very active dogs. They need regular exercise and should be given a job such as hunting or agility work. Their scenting ability is a great distraction to them, as it is with most of dogs in the Sporting Group. They can be quite stubborn and driven, because of their strong hunting instinct. This will make the recall command a difficult one to teach.

English Setters are usually quite good with children and are generally friendly to strangers after an initial period of investigation. They make excellent jogging partners, given their lithe, athletic build. Early obedience training is essential to contain their busy personality and their distractable nature. They can be horrid barkers if left alone for long periods.

Best Home: A house with a fenced yard is mandatory. Children should be taught to respect the dog and should not be allowed to wrestle or chase it. The owner of an English Setter should be an active, patient, firm leader who regularly gives the dog a task such as hunting, agility work, or tracking. Early obedience training is mandatory. The English Setter may be too active a breed for the elderly or disabled. If you are looking for a quiet, easygoing pet, an English Setter is not the dog for you.

Setter, Gordon

Origins: These beautiful setters date back to seventeenth-century Scotland, where they were valued for their pointing, retrieving, and tracking ability.

Appearance: The Gordon Setter stands 23 to 27 inches at the shoulder and weighs between 45 and 70 pounds. It has a graceful, solid, athletic body. Its shedding coat is of medium length, is lustrous and wavy, and needs a daily brushing. The coat is always black-and-tan.

Breed Profile: This beautiful, graceful breed is more serious and sensitive than its clownish cousin, the Irish Setter. Gordons tend to be on the shy side; they are often reserved and suspicious of strangers. They are of average intelligence and bond closely with their owners. They can be good with their owners' children, provided they don't roughhouse. They may not be as amiable with the children's friends, however. But they are good watchdogs.

Gordons are active dogs that need plenty of exercise. They make great jogging partners because of their leggy, agile build.

Gordon Setters can be difficult to train. They learn rather slowly, and if they are pressed too hard, they may become passive-resistant, taking a "head in the sand" attitude, or they may show aggression, depending on the intensity of the training. Always go slow with a Gordon, and be clear about what you are asking the dog to do. Allow more time for a Gordon to learn whatever you are teaching, and don't use overbearing techniques.

Some Gordon Setters have a tendency toward fear-based aggression toward people or dogs, so make sure yours is amply socialized from the first day. Take your dog to friends' homes, shopping centers, and parks, but avoid any off-leash dogs that might scare your puppy. Introduce your puppy to as many people and animals as possible when it is young and impressionable.

Best Home: A house with a fenced yard is essential. The Gordon Setter is an active dog and should be with active people. Older children are okay provided they are respectful and not rough. Regular exercise is essential for a Gordon; jogging or field work would be helpful. Obedience training and socialization are necessities for this breed and must not be hurried. Left alone too long, the Gordon may become vocal and destructive. The elderly and disabled may have trouble providing the Gordon Setter with enough exercise.

Setter, Irish

Origins: The red-and-white Irish Setter first appeared in Ireland in the late eighteenth century. It was perfected as the dog we know today in the nineteenth century. Though originally used as a gun dog, this breed now does little hunting in the United States and is predominantly a companion dog.

Appearance: The Irish Setter stands 21 to 25 inches at the shoulder and weighs between 55 and 70 pounds. It has the agile, sleek build of an athlete. The long, silky, medium to long shedding coat requires a daily brushing. This dog is a deep chestnut color and is one of the most beautiful breeds. It may need a touch-up clipping every few months.

Breed Profile: This breed has a flamboyant personality to match its coloration. Irish Setters are real clowns and can be exasperating to train. They are friendly, zany, pushy, and independent-minded, and will constantly test your patience. Irish Setters are good with children and strangers and, though easily distracted and not overly bright, are nevertheless much more resilient under the pressures of training than are Gordon Setters. Irish Setters can be noisy and will want to stick their noses where they don't belong. They are very active, busy dogs; the elderly and infirm will not be able to keep up with them. Irish Setters need a lot of exercise; if left alone too long or not exercised, they can be quite destructive. Give them a job to do; direct their impetuous nature.

Best Home: A house with a fenced yard is mandatory for this athletic, high-strung breed. Children are fine, provided no roughhousing or chasing is allowed. The owner of an Irish Setter must be a firm leader, but must also be patient, for this is not the most intelligent of breeds. You should be an athletic owner; joggers could not find a better partner to run with. The elderly and the disabled should pass on this breed. Owners of Irish Setters must begin obedience training early. The Come command may be difficult to teach because of the Irish Setters' inquisitive nature and excellent nose, which constantly leads them astray.

Spaniel, American Water

Origins: This versatile hunting dog was developed in the nineteenth century in the midwestern United States in response to the need for a dog that could retrieve, swim, track, and flush. The breed resulted from the mixing of Irish Water Spaniel and Curly-Coated Retriever bloodlines.

Appearance: The American Water Spaniel stands 15 to 18 inches at the shoulder and weighs between 25 and 45 pounds. The shedding, all-weather coat consists of tight curls. This agile dog is liver-colored and needs periodic clipping.

Breed Profile: Like all hunting breeds, American Water Spaniels are energetic. They have a good nose, are strong swimmers, can flush game, and retrieve well. Though similar in appearance to the Irish Water Spaniel, the American Water Spaniel is not as large and not quite as clownish. These dogs can be quite suspicious of strangers and will be territorial around the home. Without proper socialization from an early age, this breed can be timid around new people and in new situations. Though of a manageable size, their activity level and keen sense of smell make them a challenge to train and keep as house pets.

American Water Spaniels may be possessive of food and toys, like most spaniels. This must be dealt with from the time the dog is a puppy; you must establish leadership early on, letting the puppy know that you have the right to handle its food dish and toys whenever you wish.

Best Home: A house with a fenced yard is essential. The owner of an American Water Spaniel needs to be a patient leader and must not spoil the dog, for fear of encouraging the possessive aggression so common to spaniels. Though relatively small, this very active dog is not suitable for the elderly or the disabled. This breed may not do well with small children. Older children should be fine around this spaniel, as long as they are not permitted to roughhouse. Socialization and training must start early and must be consistent and not overbearing.

Spaniel, Clumber

Origins: The Clumber Spaniel was developed in early nineteenth-century England and France. It is thought that the Basset Hound and some early spaniel types were mixed to produce this powerful, slower-moving breed known for its endurance and its excellent sense of smell. The Clumber's strength enables it to move well through dense brush in pursuit of game.

Appearance: The Clumber Spaniel stands 17 to 20 inches at the shoulder and weighs 55 to 85 pounds. Its low-riding body is heavy and strong, with a thicker-boned structure than the other spaniels. Its shedding weather-resistant coat is thick, straight, and soft and easily absorbs odors, necessitating regular grooming and periodic clipping. The color is white with lemon markings. The Clumber's tail is docked.

Breed Profile: The Clumber Spaniel, though bigger, slower, and less energetic than the other spaniels, is still an active breed. It is normally good with its family members, though it may be suspicious of strangers and may not tolerate small children roughhousing with it. Like most spaniels, the Clumber tends to be possessive of food and toys. This must be addressed from the time the dog is a puppy; the owner must handle the dog's food bowl and possessions regularly and must establish unquestionable leadership from day one.

Because of their obstinate nature and their incredible scenting ability (both traits inherited from the Basset Hound), Clumbers are easily distracted by smells and will ignore you completely if you don't start training early. They are therefore a challenge to trainers.

The recall command is particularly hard to teach to a Clumber, or to any other breed possessing an acute sense of smell.

It is important not to let this breed become overweight, due to its long back and short legs. Obese Clumbers can develop back, hip, leg, and wrist problems. They can also be susceptible to ear infections, so clean your dog's ears at least once a week. Entropion, a folding in of the eyelids, can also occur in this breed. This can be treated only through surgery. Watch out for tear duct infections as well.

Best Home: Though this breed can live in an apartment if given daily exercise, the Clumber is better off in a house with a fenced yard. The owner of a Clumber must be a firm leader and must not spoil the dog, for fear of increasing its tendency toward possessive aggression. Older children should be taught not to wrestle or roughhouse with the dog. Clumbers may not tolerate young children, who might be bitten over a possession issue. Early training and socialization are crucial. The elderly and the infirm might be able to live with this breed if they have adequate leadership skills.

Spaniel, Cocker

Origins: First developed in nineteenth-century England, the Cocker Spaniel was originally used to flush the woodcock, a popular game bird. The dog's small size allowed it to penetrate dense brush in areas that were all but inaccessible to the larger sporting breeds. The Cocker is rarely used for hunting now and is considered primarily a companion dog.

Appearance: The Cocker Spaniel is the smallest of the sporting dogs, standing 14 to 15 inches at the shoulder and weighing 25 to 35 pounds. These dogs have a long, high-maintenance coat that mats easily and readily absorbs odors, necessitating regular bathing, brushing, and grooming. The coat may be black, ASCOB (any solid color other than black), or parti-color (two or more colors, one of which is always white).

Breed Profile: Few dogs are as cute and cuddly as the Cocker Spaniel. Unfortunately, few breeds currently pose so many problems. The popularity of this breed, like that of the Rottweiler and the Dalmatian, has given rise to a legion of substandard breeders, including puppy mill owners who supply thousands of poor-quality dogs to pet shops nationwide. As a result, the quality of Cockers has plummeted to an all-time low.

Cockers are well known for developing ear infections; they must have their ears cleaned on a regular basis in order to avoid this. They also tend to get eye and tear-duct infections. In addition, they are famous for having a submissive wetting problem that can become intolerable. Many Cockers will wet whenever they are petted.

Cockers are fairly bright, but they are also notoriously stubborn and often try to outsmart their owners. This makes them difficult to train. They can be aggressive to the point of viciousness. For this reason, we discourage families with kids from choosing this breed. Recently, a client of ours had to give up her four year-old male Cocker after he severely bit her two-year-old daughter in the face, requiring thirty-seven stitches to close the wounds. The instigation for this attack was a kiss on the nose.

We have seen variations in temperament between the color variations. The most aggressive tend to be the buff-colored Cockers, which are the most popular and therefore the most overbred. Other solid-colored Cockers are next, followed by the particolor variety. However, we have worked with some parti-colored Cockers that were sweet, even-tempered dogs.

Cockers bite. Ask your vet or groomer. Of all the breeds we work with, they top the list. We take for granted that a Cocker coming in for training may attempt to bite at least once. Families with kids should stay clear of this breed.

Cockers do not bark a lot, but they do tend to scream when resisting training or undergoing separation anxiety. They are affectionate with their owners, albeit in a controlling way. They can be decent pets for the elderly, but they won't deal well with the grandchildren.

If you choose a Cocker, be sure to select one from a reputable breeder. No pet shops! Observe the parents and the litter closely. Consider a particolor, and start obedience training and socialization right away. Make sure you handle the dog from day one, including brushing, cleaning eyes and ears, and cutting nails. Do not spoil a Cocker, do not allow it to become overweight, and stay away from pet shops!

Best Home: An apartment is fine as long as the dog is exercised daily. We strongly advise against choosing this breed if you have children. Elderly or disabled owners are fine provided they are strong leaders, can work the dog in obedience, and have no young grandchildren. Spoilers should stay away from this breed. Do not let this breed sleep in your bed, for this will unintentionally tell it that it is on equal footing with you, which will undermine your leadership. The Cocker owner must be willing to handle and groom the dog every day. Those who live in wet climates should avoid this breed, as the extremely absorbent coat can become mildewed and smelly.

Spaniel, English Cocker

Origins: The English Cocker Spaniel, a descendant of the original Spanish spaniels, first came to prominence in seventeenth-century Europe as a flusher of woodcock and other small game birds. In nineteenth- and twentieth-century America, a blurring of English and American Cockers occurred, and the English Cocker  was not defined here as a separate breed until the mid-twentieth century.

Appearance: The English Cocker stands 15 to 17 inches at the shoulder and weighs 25 to 35 pounds. The body is sturdy, robust, strong, and lankier than that of the American Cocker. The English Cocker's shedding coat is fine, wavy, and medium to long. It absorbs odors and will need regular bathing and brushing and periodic clipping. The color may be black-and-tan, particolor (black-and-white or tan-and-white), tricolor (black, tan, and white), or roan, a speckled pattern, usually of blue and white.

Breed Profile: This high-energy breed is still used for hunting, unlike its American cousin. It has not been overbred and therefore retains a more stable, consistent temperament than the American. It is normally friendly and good with children and does not show the American's tendency toward aggression. The English Cocker also does not seem to show the same degree of possessive aggression. It is usually very affectionate and often on the submissive side. It can be stubborn, however, and will not learn as quickly as some other breeds. Training must begin early, and the trainer must be patient and not overbearing. Without training, the high activity level of this breed will make it an annoying pet to live with.

Like its American cousin, the English Cocker Spaniel can be difficult to housebreak and may be a submissive wetter. It may also be prone to eye and ear infections; the ears must be cleaned every week. It is a good idea to keep this breed as dry as possible because of the odor-absorbing quality of the coat.

Best Home: A house with a fenced yard is best for this breed. Start training early, and provide the dog with daily exercise and some job to do, be it hunting, tracking, or agility work. Children are fine, provided they do not roughhouse. The elderly and the disabled can own this breed if they are able to work the dog in obedience and exercise it. The owner of an English Cocker Spaniel should be a patient leader who does not use overbearing training techniques and who will not spoil the dog.

Spaniel, English Springer

Origins: Developed in nineteenth-century England to flush, or spring, pheasants, this breed has become a popular house pet in addition to still being an important gun dog.

Appearance: The English Springer Spaniel stands 19 to 20 inches at the shoulder and weighs 42 to 55 pounds. The flat or slightly wavy coat is of moderate length, shedding little but requiring daily brushing and periodic clipping. The color may be black-and-white or liver-and-white.

Breed Profile: Few breeds puzzle us more than this one. A well-bred English Springer is a joy—attentive, hardworking, loyal, and affectionate. But this is also the breed with the highest incidence of dogs euthanized for aggression toward their owners. It is a Jekyll and Hyde story.

The aggression we see in this breed almost always arises over an issue of possessiveness, particularly over food, a favorite toy, or a sleeping place. Do not give this problem a chance to develop; from the start, make sure you can handle the puppy's food dish often. While the puppy is eating, pick up the dish, place a piece of cheese or a slice of hot dog in it, and then set it back down. This will teach the puppy that having you handle its dish is something to look forward to. Some Springers will bite their owners if the dogs are awakened too suddenly or if they are surprised in some way. This aggressive behavior often is not evident in the puppy, making it hard to predict if the adult dog will show this tendency.

Springers sometimes bond too closely with their owners and consequently suffer from separation anxiety when the owner leaves. This can result in incessant barking and destructive behavior. Remember that this sporting breed needs to release energy through regular exercise. This will help reduce stress and destructive behavior.

Do not overdo greetings and departures with this breed. Greet it the way you would a member of the family. Don't patronize the animal. The same goes for departures.

We like the personality and temperament of good English Springer Spaniels. They are intelligent and eager to please, and they do well in the obedience ring. Unfortunately, however, we cannot at this time recommend this breed for families with children; the possibility of aggression is just too high.

Best Home: A house with a fenced yard is imperative. At this time we feel that families with children should avoid this breed. Also, this is not a breed for the elderly or the disabled. The owner of an English Springer needs to be a strong leader; obedience training should start from day one. Springers are smarter than most dogs and can learn quickly. Hunters would find this breed an excellent working companion. Spoiling is taboo; this breed needs consistent rules and needs to know it is not the center of attention. Consider getting a female; the females tend to have a much lower incidence of aggression.

Spaniel, Field

Origins: A greatly manipulated breed in early nineteenth-century England, it took some time to stabilize the standard of this breed. In their attempts to breed a versatile medium-sized hunting dog, breeders initially mixed Clumber, Welsh, and Sussex Spaniels, and later English Springer and American Cocker. At the time they seemed unable to decide on the archetype. Currently the Field Spaniel is well defined and standardized.

Appearance: The Field Spaniel stands approximately 18 inches at the shoulder and weighs between 35 and 55 pounds. It has a sturdy medium-size body and a slightly wavy medium-length coat that sheds and absorbs odors, necessitating regular brushing and bathing, and an occasional touch-up clip. This breed is shorter than the English Springer but just as heavy. The coat can be black, liver, roan (a dark color with splashes of white), or red.

Breed Profile: The Field Spaniel is a slower worker than the English Springer, falling somewhere between the Clumber and the Springer in activity level. These dogs have good endurance. They are smart, have a keen sense of smell, and are good retrievers. Field Spaniels are on the timid side with people they don't know, so they need socialization from an early age. Like other spaniels, they can be possessive-aggressive over food and toys. They learn quickly, but are sensitive to overbearing training techniques. You must be firm and patient. Their sense of smell will act as a major distraction to training; though they are good retrievers, the Come command may be the hardest to perfect. They are good with considerate children, but may snap at a young child over an issue of possession. Field

Spaniels are susceptible to ear and eye infections and must have their eyes and ears inspected often and cleaned as needed.

Best Home: A house with a fenced yard is essential. Older children are okay as long as they don't roughhouse. The owner of a Field Spaniel must be firm yet patient and must start training and socialization early on. The elderly and the disabled can own this breed provided they are able to train and exercise it on a daily basis.

Spaniel, Irish Water

Origins: This is a very old breed, dating back to seventh- and eighth-century Ireland. The breed as we know it was perfected by the eighteenth century. The Irish Water Spaniel, though capable of flushing birds like other spaniels, was actually bred to excel as a water retriever.

Appearance: The Irish Water Spaniel is the largest of the spaniels, standing 21 to 24 inches at the shoulder and weighing 45 to 65 pounds. It has a strong physique and a dense, curly, water-resistant coat that sheds little but requires regular brushing and periodic clipping. This agile breed is known for its topknot of curls and its ratlike tail. The coat is liver-colored.

Breed Profile: The Irish Water Spaniel is an excellent water dog and retriever. It is a very active, precocious dog, known for its clownish, testing personality. These dogs are curious and expressive, active, somewhat stubborn, and independent. They can be suspicious of strangers and can be aggressive toward other dogs. Irish Water Spaniels tend to be very good watch dogs. Socialization and obedience training need to begin at an early age.

Irish Water Spaniels love to work and need to be given some job to do, whether it be field work, tracking, obedience, or agility. They are loyal to their owners and do not exhibit the possessive-aggressive problems seen in some other spaniels. Irish Water Spaniels can be susceptible to hip dysplasia and hypothyroidism.

Best Home: A house with a fenced yard is preferable. These dogs need strong leadership from early on; they will walk all over a spoiling, weak leader. They should be socialized with people and dogs from puppyhood. They are usually safe with children, provided no roughhousing occurs.

This is a breed that needs to be given a task; it will be restless if not given adequate direction. The elderly and the disabled might have trouble keeping up with this breed.

Spaniel, Sussex

Origins: The Sussex Spaniel, first seen in nineteenth-century England, was bred to hunt where game was plentiful and speed was not essential. The Sussex Spaniel did not become a popular hunting dog in the United States because of the more expansive terrain, which required a faster dog.

Appearance: The Sussex Spaniel stands 16 to 18 inches at the shoulder and weighs between 35 and 45 pounds. It is long in the back, short-legged, thick-bodied, and thick-boned. It has a wavy, absorbent medium-length coat that sheds seasonally and that can mat and get dirty easily. It requires daily brushing, periodic bathing, and an occasional clipping. The color is always a light shade of liver. The tail is docked.

Breed Profile: This active breed is a good hunter and retriever with good scenting ability. Sussex Spaniels are friendly, but they may be initially reserved around strangers and they will not tolerate rough-housing from children. They can be difficult to train because of their scenting ability and their level of activity, which may cause them to be easily distracted. Sussex Spaniels can be obstinate and should receive obedience training and socialization early on. They can also be quite noisy, producing an almost Basset-like bay that may not sit well with neighbors.

We have seen the possessive-aggression problem in this breed. Sussex Spaniels must have consistent leadership from the start and must not be spoiled or taught any chase or keep-away games. Sussex Spaniels can be hard to housebreak and may suffer from ear infections and eye discharge. The ears and eyes should be checked daily and cleaned when necessary.

A Sussex Spaniel, though not as active as a Springer or an Irish Water Spaniel, is nevertheless a high-energy dog that must be given exercise. Obedience work, hunting, tracking, or agility work will help focus this dog and give it a sense of accomplishment.

Best Home: A house with a fenced yard is essential. Older children should be fine, as long as they do not harass or play chase or keep-away games with the dog. The owner of a Sussex must be a competent leader and have time to exercise and groom the dog daily. Without exercise and some structured activity this sporting breed may become loud and destructive. Early obedience training and socialization are mandatory. Elderly or disabled persons might get by with this breed if they can provide the necessary leadership and exercise. Spoiling this dog could lead to possessive-aggression problems.

Spaniel, Welsh Springer

Origins: This spaniel, which first appeared in seventeenth- and eighteenth-century Wales, was bred for its birding ability and its adaptability to varied climates and conditions.

Appearance: The Welsh Springer Spaniel stands 16 to 17 inches at the shoulder and weighs 35 to 45 pounds. Its body size is somewhere between that of a Cocker and an English Springer. The medium-length seasonally shedding coat is straight and silky with an undercoat. It requires periodic brushing and trimming. The Welsh has a docked tail.

Breed Profile: This is a happy, affectionate, energetic dog that has a more sensitive personality than the English Springer. Welsh Springers can be initially timid around strangers and need socialization early on. The owner must be patient and consistent with this breed; no heavy-handed techniques should be used. Training should be started early, and daily exercise is mandatory. Like all of the sporting breeds, Welsh Springers do best when given a job to do, such as retrieving, hunting, tracking, or agility. If not exercised, they can become restless and destructive. Though we have not seen a significant level of possessive aggression in this breed, the possibility does exist. Strong, patient leadership combined with clear consistent rules and no teasing keep-away games should help curb this.

Best Home: A house with a fenced yard is essential. Children are fine provided they don't roughhouse. The owner of a Welsh Springer should be a patient, strong leader who has time to work in obedience and to socialize the dog from early on. This breed also needs a job, be it hunting, retrieving, or agility work. Do not spoil this breed. Cautious, nervous people should avoid this breed. The elderly and disabled can own this breed provided they obedience train the dog.

Vizsla

Origins: This hunting dog, which first appeared in Central Europe in the thirteenth and fourteenth centuries, was used to locate and flush birds for falconers, whose trained birds of prey would then bring the hunted birds down. The Vizsla's short coat allowed it to be used in the warmer climates of southern Hungary. With the advent of firearms, the Vizsla became adept at pointing and retrieving game.

Appearance: The Vizsla stands 21 to 24 inches at the shoulder and weighs between 45 and 60 pounds. It has a short, low-maintenance shedding coat. The color is a rich rust. The tail is docked.

Breed Profile: This is an active, playful, happy, alert hunting breed with a personality somewhere between that of a Pointer and a spaniel. It is sensitive yet stubborn, a combination that makes training a challenge. Like the Pointer, the Vizsla can be easily distracted by scent and may choose to ignore your commands if an interesting smell presents itself.

The Vizsla can be timid around strangers and so must be socialized early on. It is usually fine with other dogs and with children, so long as no roughhousing occurs. Some Vizslas can be hard to housebreak and can be submissive wetters.

The Vizsla needs early obedience training to overcome a tendency toward nonthinking hyperactivity. The Come command is especially important, as it is with any breed with strong scenting ability. The training must be firm but never harsh and must be meted out more slowly than with a spaniel, for the Vizsla is not quite as bright. Daily exercise is mandatory; without it, this breed will become restless and destructive. Its lean, muscular body makes it the perfect jogging partner. Any kind of retrieving, field, or agility work will help direct this active breed's energies and is recommended.

Best Home: The Vizsla needs to live in a house with a fenced yard. It doesn't do well in the city. It needs daily exercise and perhaps a job such as hunting, retrieving, or agility work. A hunter or jogger would enjoy this breed. Cold climates are not the best for this short-coated breed. Children are fine as long as they don't roughhouse. The owner of a Vizsla must be patient yet firm, and must enjoy a dog with boundless energy. Harsh training techniques will ruin the dog. A Vizsla owner must have time to train and socialize this breed, which can be destructive and noisy if left alone for long periods. The elderly and disabled should avoid this active breed.

Weimaraner

Origins: This fairly new breed first appeared in late nine-teenth-century Germany. The Bloodhound and various pointer types were mixed to produce a hunting dog with superior scenting ability, agility, speed, and strength. Weimaraners were originally used to hunt large game such as the wolf and bear, but they are now used primarily as bird dogs.

Appearance: The Weimaraner stands 23 to 27 inches at the shoulder and weighs 55 to 90 pounds. It has a strong muscular body with a deep chest, and is more athletic and powerful than a Pointer. The shedding coat is a very short metallic gray and easy to maintain. The tail is docked. The Weimaraner's eyes are a unique amber color.

Breed Profile: The Weimaraner is similar to the Pointer in temperament. It is a big, high-energy dog that is high-strung and easily distracted by scent. This breed is like a racing machine constantly revving its engine. It is as sensitive as a sight hound but as stubborn and driven as a scent hound. This makes it a challenge to train.

The Weimaraner, especially a male, can be very dominant and territorial and can also be reserved and suspicious of strangers. It needs to be socialized early on. It can be good with your own older children but may inadvertently knock down and hurt smaller children. Its level of energy is so high that it can wear out an unsuspecting owner. This breed was designed for a special purpose, namely hunting. In our opinion it does not make the jump to family pet so easily. The owner of this breed must give it a task such as hunting and provide it with daily exercise. Joggers do well with this athletic breed. If left in a yard all day, however, a Weimaraner can become noisy, destructive, and very territorial. If you leave a Weimaraner inside all day, you may come home to find your house chewed to ribbons. The key is early, patient, firm training, supervision, and lots of exercise.

Best Home: A house with a fenced yard or a fenced kennel is essential. A hunter would love this breed. It is tireless and driven and has a remarkable sense of smell. The owner of a Weimaraner must be a strong, no-nonsense leader with time to train, socialize, and exercise the dog. The owner must also be able to tolerate a very busy, high-energy dog. Do not expect this breed to lie at your feet while you read the paper. Older children are fine provided no roughhousing occurs. The elderly and disabled should avoid this powerful high-strung breed.

Wirehaired Pointing Griffon

Origins: This breed, which
first appeared in late nineteenth-century Holland and
France, was created by mixing
Otterhound and German
Shorthaired Pointer bloodlines. It filled the need for a
versatile hunter that could
point and retrieve on land or
in the water. The rough coat
served as protection against
wet, cold weather and harsh thickets.

Appearance: The Wirehaired Pointing Griffon stands 20 to 24
inches at the shoulder and weighs between 50 and 65 pounds. It
has a solid, robust physique and a wiry, rough, medium-length shedding coat that requires periodic brushing. The color is gray with
brown and some white markings. The tail is docked.

Breed Profile: This is an active breed that exhibits pointer-like behavior but has a terrierlike attitude. It is easily distracted by scent
and can be very resistant to obedience training. It is a good watchdog and may be suspicious of strangers. It will accept older children, but may not tolerate younger children or any kind of
roughhousing. Early training is needed to counteract this breed's
passive-resistant a head-in-the-sand attitude toward obedience. The
Come command is difficult to master because of the scent-
distraction potential. This breed must be socialized early on to minimize fear of strangers, and it must be given plenty of exercise daily.

Best Home: A house with a fenced yard is essential. Hunters would
find this dog a superb worker. Older, respectful children are okay.
The owner of a Wirehaired Pointing Griffon should be a strong,
active, confident, patient leader who desires a high-energy dog to

use for hunting or some other outside activity. Nurturing, cautious owners should stay clear of this breed, as should the elderly and the disabled. If this breed is left alone for too long, it may become noisy and destructive. The owner must have time for training and exercise. The Wirehaired Pointing Griffon would make a good jogging partner, but not in a hot climate. This is not the dog for someone who is looking for an easygoing foot-warmer.

The Hound Group

The Hound Group includes both scent hounds and sight hounds. Scent hounds, such as the Beagle, track prey by using their sense of smell. They are high-energy dogs and tend to be very driven and devoted to their appointed task of finding the prey. They are hard to obedience-train because of this attribute. Sight hounds, such as the Greyhound, spot their prey visually and then run it down. They are fleet of foot, slow to learn, and somewhat aloof with strangers. Sight hounds are more sensitive to anesthesia than other breeds.

Afghan Hound

Origins: An ancient breed, the Afghan Hound was used in mountainous Afghanistan and northern India as a coursing hound. It would spot its prey— rabbits or gazelles—and then run them down, independent of the hunter, who would arrive on horseback after the capture. The Afghan's long coat allowed it to stay warm in the

harsh climate of Afghanistan, something that its faster, short-haired cousin from Egypt, the Greyhound, would not have been able to do.

Appearance: The Afghan Hound stands 25 to 27 inches at the shoulder and weighs between 50 and 60 pounds. The body is lithe, athletic, and capable of supple, agile movement. The shedding coat is long, silky, and hard to maintain. It absorbs moisture and odors and requires a daily brushing and regular clipping. It is advisable to keep the coat dry. The feet and ears are feathered, and there is a topknot of long silky hair. The color may be silver, cream, black, brindle, black-and-tan, or a combination of shades.

Breed Profile: This fast, agile sight hound is aloof, dignified, and rather snooty with all but its close family. It is very independent and aristocratic by nature and will be reserved and suspicious of strangers. It is not a great family dog and will not tolerate boisterous children or uninvited attention. It may shy away from the unwanted petting hand of a stranger.

The Afghan is very laid-back at home, however, happily curling up on a sofa or on a sheepskin and idling the day away. Nevertheless, it does need to get out and run on a regular basis.

Training is difficult with this breed. Sensitive and not overly bright, the Afghan will balk if pushed too quickly. It processes information more slowly than other breeds. Your training technique must therefore be clear, slow, and precise. Overbearing methods will serve only to panic the breed and possibly bring on fearful snapping. As with most sight hounds, the Sit and Come commands take an especially long time to teach.

The Afghan needs to be socialized from an early age so as to limit its aloof, distrustful nature. This is not a breed to spoil or pamper, despite its beauty and its haughty nature. Spoiling will enhance a dominant attitude and increase the chances of aggression. This breed can also be small dog-aggressive and has a very high prey drive toward smaller animals.

Best Home: The owner of an Afghan Hound should be an easy-going person who does not demand constant interaction with the dog. Owning an Afghan or any other sight hound is similar to owning a cat; it does not always desire affection. If you are expecting Lab-type allegiance and attention, forget about this breed.

The Afghan is generally quiet and lazy most of the time and so can live in the city or in an apartment. The owner must run this breed regularly, however, and this can be difficult in the city, as few fenced areas are big enough to allow it room to really open up.

Joggers do well with this breed, as long as the dog is socialized well enough to tolerate bikes and joggers quickly going by. The Afghan does not interact well with children. The elderly and disabled might have trouble exercising this active breed.

This breed should not be left outside all day, because of the absorbency of its coat and because of the breed's ability to easily jump a six-foot fence. Fortunately the Afghan Hound does quite well indoors.

Basenji

Origins: The Basenji traces its lineage back to Egyptian times. This breed was used for ratting, retrieving, and chasing game into nets. Today it is primarily a companion dog.

Appearance: The Basenji stand 16 to 17 inches at the shoulder and weighs between 20 and 28 pounds. It has a small, sturdy, muscular build. Its shedding coat is short, lustrous, and low-maintenance, requiring only periodic brushing. The color may be red-and-white, black-and-tan, black with white markings, or brindle. This breed cleans itself, so bathing is rarely necessary. The Basenji has very little body fat, and so the owner should provide a blanket or sheepskin for it to lie on. It has a curiously wrinkled brow, giving it a thoughtful, pensive look.

Breed Profile: The Basenji is a unique breed and is behaviorally and physically unlike the other sight hounds. Though it can be as aloof as the others, it has a sassier, more obstinate, and more out-going temperament. Cocky, proud, and vain, it is aware of its uniqueness, playing it to the hilt. Its early use as a ratter and vermin chaser makes its original purpose closer to that of a terrier than a sight hound, which may explain its sassier nature. Basenji bitches come into season only once a year, unlike the other breeds, which have a twice-a-year cycle. This may be a throwback to wild ancestry, where bitches had only one heat per year.

Behaviorally, this breed is, shall we say, dynamic. Though bark-less, a Basenji is by no means silent. Its vocalizations range from a pleasant chortling to a horrific screaming wail emitted during its infamous bouts of stubbornness, which occur when you ask it to sit or, heaven forbid, lie down. A young Basenji may go into a vocal tirade whenever you have the audacity to leave it home alone. It can also be quite destructive if left alone for long periods of time. For this reason, it doesn't always make a good apartment pet. On the positive side, the Basenji is a very clean dog and spends much of its time preening like a cat.

The Basenji can be extremely dominant and stubborn and is likely to resist obedience training more than most breeds. Proud and cocky, it won't willingly recognize a leader. One of our hardest tasks as trainers is to get a Basenji to lie down and stay, or to come when called. The look on its face makes its thought clear: "You *can't* be talking to *me.*" During bouts of stubbornness, it is possible for this breed to show aggression, and somewhere along the line a Basenji may attempt to nip or bite. For this, reason, we don't rec-ommend the Basenji for families with children or for households where unpredictable commotion occurs. Unlike a Greyhound, which would probably go into another room to escape the chaos, a Basenji will say, "Hey, knock it off!" It is also very likely, without any vocal warning, to bite a stranger who reaches down to pet it.

Despite its behavioral problems, we confess a grudging respect for this breed. The Basenji has plenty of personality and can be a fascinating character.

Best Home: An apartment is adequate provided the dog is walked each day. Bear in mind, however, that Basenjis can be very noisy, especially during training. The owner should be a strong, patient leader who has the courage to deal with doggy temper tantrums. Don't spoil this breed, for heaven's sake!

If you choose a Basenji, always keep it on leash out of doors, and don't expect it to tolerate strangers or other dogs.

We recommend against choosing this breed if you have children. Any roughhousing may result in a child being bitten.

The elderly and the disabled may have trouble establishing leadership with a Basenji.

The owner of a Basenji must make time for regular training and socialization and must be firm and resolute. This breed will challenge your authority and will walk all over you if you pamper it.

One last point: if you keep a Basenji in an outdoor kennel, be sure to have the runs securely covered—Basenjis can climb fences as skillfully a monkeys.

Basset Hound

Origins: First used in sixteenth- and seventeenth-century France for deer and rabbit tracking, the Basset Hound was designed for use in dense cover. Its short legs allow it to enter tight spots that would be inaccessible to the larger scent hounds, and its slowness ensures that it won't overrun the scent. Its phenomenal nose and its ability to hunt  in a pack have made it an invaluable hunting companion.

Appearance: The Basset Hound stands 14 to 15 inches at the shoulder and weighs between 50 and 70 pounds. Heavy-boned and thick-bodied, it has a long back, short, thick legs, and very long ears. The shedding coat is short and low-maintenance, requiring only a periodic brushing. The coloring is usually a mixture of white, black, and tan.

Breed Profile: Like other scent hounds, the Basset can be stubborn and driven, constantly distracted by smells we cannot even imagine. Its scenting ability is second only to that of the Bloodhound, and serves as the great preoccupation in its life.

Like the Bloodhound and the Black-and-Tan Coonhound, the Basset has a potential for aggression when pushed too hard. This aggression, when it occurs, is a non-thinking response for a Basset and can be hard to modify. It always comes as a surprise to the owner, because Bassets are normally lazy, sluggish, affectionate dogs. When a Basset decides to follow a scent, however, it objects strongly to any interference and is capable of seriously biting its owner or anyone else who gets in its way.

A Basset can be suspicious of strangers and makes a good watchdog. Unfortunately, it is not too tolerant of children. We have had numerous incidents of Bassets doing harm to small children.

The Basset needs obedience training and socialization early on. It is not an extremely bright breed; training should be consistent and patient. Sitting is an uncomfortable position for this dog because of its short legs and long back, so don't require it to hold a Sit for very long. The Come command is very difficult with any scent hound because scent acts as a narcotic on them. Once a Basset picks up a scent, responding to an owner's Come command is the farthest thing from the dog's mind.

We advise against having two Bassets, particularly two males from the same litter.

The Basset is noisy. It bays and has a big-dog bark. It will also snore.

Several physical problems need to be mentioned. Bassets are prone to structural problems, including arthritis in the neck, back, hips, and legs. Pain can cause aggression in any dog, and this breed is very susceptible. Make sure you minimize this problem by keeping the dog's weight in check and providing regular but not intense exercise; do not jog with a Basset. This breed may also develop ear infections; the ears should be cleaned regularly. Start doing this when the dog is a puppy or you will risk getting bitten. It is also important to clip a Basset's toenails frequently; long toenails can cause a distortion of the foot placement, eventually resulting in ankle problems.

Best Home: A house with a fenced yard is preferable. This is not a breed for families with children. The owner of a Basset Hound must be a firm yet patient leader and must have time to train and socialize the dog. If you spoil this breed, you risk creating a biter, so don't do it. The elderly and the disabled must be able to train and exercise this strong breed if they desire to own one. Joggers should not consider this breed, as extended running can damage the dog's back, legs, and hips.

Beagle

Origins: The beginnings of this breed, which may have originated in medieval England, are hazy. Used as a fast, agile tracker of fox and rabbit, the Beagle was bred to have great scenting ability and to hunt in a pack. Its small size gave it access to brush that was impenetrable to the Foxhound.

Appearance: Beagles, which are among the smaller scent hounds, come in two varieties: one stands approximately 13 inches at the shoulder, and the other is more than 13 but not exceeding 15 inches. The Beagle will weigh between 18 and 30 pounds, depending on which height variety you have. This is a sturdy, attractive, high-energy dog with a short, low-maintenance shedding coat. The coloring is usually a mixture of tan, black, and white.

Breed Profile: Bred to track fox, the Beagle has a great nose and, like other scent hounds, will ignore you and everything else when on scent. Though affectionate and intelligent, it requires training from day one because of its stubborn nature and distractability. You will see few scent hounds, including Beagles, in the obedience ring because their nose often overrules their brain.

The Beagle, like other scent hounds, was bred to bark, bay, and howl to alert the hunter to its location during the hunt. Because this vocalization is instinctive, the Beagle may not make a good apartment pet. We actually have had clients evicted because their Beagles howled for hours while the owners were at work. On the positive side, this breed is good with children and will take lots of handling from them. It is also friendly with strangers and other dogs.

The Beagle may run away and is not likely to come when called, so you will need a secure fence that it cannot get under or over. Always keep it on leash; otherwise it may take off the minute it picks up a scent. When on scent, the dog will block out all else, including a speeding car or hungry Great Dane.

This is a very affectionate breed that is easy to pamper and nurture, but you must not spoil your Beagle. We see fat, spoiled Beagles all the time, and we find them to have separation anxiety problems and a potential for biting when pushed. This seems to be a learned behavior rather than heredity, however. Small, cute spoiled dogs very often become biters because spoiling, in a dog's mind, is what subordinates do to a leader, and it is the leader's right to discipline (bite). When you make any dog the center of attention, you tell it that it is dominant, and that is the beginning of all sorts of problems.

Best Home: A house with a fenced yard is preferable. A Beagle will be noisy and will get you in trouble if you live in an apartment. The Beagle is fine with children and strangers as long as it is not spoiled. Daily exercise is important. The owner of a Beagle must have the time to train early on and must want a breed that is active and inquisitive. The elderly and the disabled can own this breed provided they are able to obedience-train and exercise it.

Black and Tan Coonhound

Origins: First used in Medieval England, the Black and Tan Coonhound was perfected in the southern United States as a tracker of opossum, raccoon, and bear.

Appearance: Standing 23 to 27 inches at the shoulder and weighing between 70 and 90 pounds, this is a big, strong, agile scent hound. The shedding coat is short, dense, and low-maintenance, requiring only periodic brushing.

Breed Profile: This is a very active, driven breed that is primarily a hunting dog and should not be considered for use as a family pet. The Black and Tan is not as adaptable to the home as the Beagle or Basset. It is best owned by a hunter who can put its natural abilities to the best use.

The Black and Tan is ruled by a superb sense of smell and will be easily distracted by any scent wafting through the neighborhood. Like the Bloodhound and, to a lesser extent, the Basset, this breed can be provoked to aggression if required to obey when it doesn't want to or when it doesn't understand what it's expected to do. This is an explosive, non-thinking type of aggression that comes with little warning.

The instinct to track in this breed is usually stronger than an owner's ability to control; the dog goes into a driven, trance-like state that is hard to break through.

The Black and Tan Coonhound is normally suspicious of strangers, and is not recommended for families with children because of its potential for aggression. Though bred to be a pack hunter, it can be very dog-aggressive. The Coonhound is also very vocal, making it best suited to life on a farm or in the country.

The Black and Tan is susceptible to ear infections and must have its ears cleaned regularly. To accomplish this, the owner must handle the dog liberally from day one or risk being bitten. This breed is also susceptible to hip dysplasia.

Best Home: A house with a fenced yard or a kennel is essential. We feel this breed does not make a good family pet; a Coonhound does not understand and will not tolerate children, and does much better if owned and used by a hunter on a regular basis. Regular exercise is essential, as is supervision and firm no-nonsense leadership. Obedience training and socialization from day one are necessary. The elderly and the disabled should avoid this powerful, active breed, and so should anyone with a pampering or spoiling nature.

Bloodhound

Origins: This scent hound is an old breed, dating back to Roman times. It was perfected in medieval Europe, but its greatest use has come in the United States as a tracker of fugitives and lost individuals. It has the most powerful sense of smell of all the breeds.

Appearance: The Bloodhound stands 24 to 26 inches at the shoulder and weighs between 90 and 110 pounds. This is a large, powerful animal with great stamina and drive. The shedding coat is short, requiring only periodic brushing. The color may be black-and-tan, red-and-tan, or all tan. Bloodhounds have loose, wrinkled skin and long ears.

Breed Profile: The Bloodhound is known to be the best tracker of all the scent hounds. It is truly phenomenal at picking up a scent and following it relentlessly until the prey is located. The Bloodhound is a highly specialized dog bred to a narrow purpose, and its purpose is not to serve as a house pet. More than any other breed, the Bloodhound is specifically designed to perform a single task: tracking. To that end, breeders have created not only a dog with the best nose in the business but also a dog with a relentless, determined mind-set. The Bloodhound will follow a scent forever and ignore everything else, including you. "Sit"? Did you say "Sit"? You can't be serious! There's a Cocker Spaniel bitch in season eight miles down the road. Get real. See you later. Choosing a Bloodhound for a family pet would be like using a bulldozer to drive to the corner store. The application is absurd. This is a textbook example of breed-specific behavior determining a breed's niche. More than any other breed, the Bloodhound needs to perform the task for which it was bred.

Contrary to what most sources have said about the temperament of this breed, we have seen some very aggressive Bloodhounds, and in not one case were we able to permanently turn the dog around. The relentless, determined, non-thinking mind-set that is so effective in tracking can be transformed into aggressive behavior as well. And we repeat: when a Bloodhound becomes aggressive, it is almost impossible to stop. Keep in mind this is a very big dog.

The Bloodhound needs obedience training and socialization early in life. It is stubborn and is easily distracted by scents that you cannot perceive.

We don't recommend the Bloodhound as a family pet. There are exceptions to every rule, of course, but in our opinion this breed should be left to hunters, police departments, and search-and-rescue teams.

Best Home: Let us say once again that we recommend this breed for hunters, trackers, police departments, and rescue teams. Though there are always exceptions, we don't feel this breed does well with families. It can be intolerant of children and may bite if teased or provoked. The Bloodhound needs to live in the country and requires a fenced yard or kennel. The owner must be a strong, no-nonsense leader and must use this breed to do the work it was bred for.

Borzoi

Origins: These large sight hounds, once known as Russian Wolfhounds, were owned by the Russian nobility during medieval times and were bred as coursing hounds to chase rabbits, foxes, and wolves in packs. The Borzoi's speed, agility, and strength allowed it to range far ahead of the mounted hunter, acquire the prey by sight, run it down, and hold it at bay until the hunter arrived. The long coat was developed to protect the dog during the cruel Russian winter.

Appearance: The Borzoi stands 26 to 28 inches at the shoulder and weighs 65 to 100 pounds. It has a lean, leggy, athletic body and a long, silky, shedding coat of medium maintenance, requiring regular brushing and an occasional touch-up clipping. The coat is usually white with black, tan, or lemon markings.

Breed Profile: This is a typical sight hound. The Borzoi is fast, agile, aloof, and reserved with strangers. Dignified and quiet, it is also very clean. Usually close with only its immediate family, it may not welcome petting from strangers. The Borzoi is normally intolerant of unpredictable young children, and cornered, it may bite without warning.

The Borzi needs early training and socialization. The training should not be overbearing, as the Borzoi tends to process information slowly and will shut down if pushed. Patience and consistency are important. The Sit command is difficult to teach because of the Borzoi's bony, lanky structure and lack of body padding. The Come command is essential and must be perfected, because the Borzoi's great speed enables it to disappear from sight in seconds.

The Borzoi has a high prey drive and will seize and kill small animals before you can react. It can also be very dog-aggressive.

Like all sight hounds, the Borzoi must often be allowed time to be by itself. Don't expect it to be as affectionate as a Lab or a Golden Retriever. It won't have a "pet me, love me" attitude. Owners who are used to the mind-set of cats will appreciate this breed—but it would be a mistake to own a cat along with a Borzoi.

Borzoi's need a bed or a blanket to lie on. They don't have much muscle or fat on their bodies, and they can get pressure sores if their sleeping area is not cushioned properly.

Best Home: An apartment is okay provided the Borzoi is exercised daily. A quiet environment free of unpredictable events and young children is preferred. Small animals may pose a problem due to this breed's high prey drive.

A Borzoi needs to run. This will be possible only if you have properly trained the dog to come when called and if you have socialized it among other dogs and people. Again, keep in mind that, your Borzoi may attack a small dog if it is allowed off-leash.

Borzoi owners should be calm, easygoing leaders who do not necessarily want a dog to be in their face all the time. Nervous, hyperactive, and pampering types should avoid this breed. The elderly and disabled may have trouble exercising this breed. A Borzoi should not be left alone in a yard, for it can easily jump a six-foot fence. It will be happier inside the home, as are most breeds. Owners must also make time for obedience training and early socialization.

Dachshund

Origins: Used as a tracker of badger in medieval Europe, this breed was once larger than it is today. It was bred down in size to hunt foxes and rabbits. It has an excellent sense of smell and a scrappy, almost terrier-like temperament that allowed it to tangle with its sometimes difficult prey.

Appearance: The Dachshund comes in two sizes: standard and miniature. The standard-size Dachshund is approximately 9 inches tall at the shoulder and weighs 12 to 24 pounds. The miniature stands 5 to 6 inches at the shoulder and weighs under 12 pounds. Occurring in both size variations are three coat types: smooth, longhaired, and wirehaired. The smooth coat is short, glossy, and shedding and requires little maintenance. The longhaired coat, also shedding, is of medium length, shiny, silky, slightly wavy, and of low maintenance, requiring brushing twice a week. The wirehaired coat is rougher and harder, almost terrierlike in texture, medium-length, and shedding. Colors are chestnut

brown, black-and-tan, and a mixture of other colors.

Dogs of both sizes are long-backed and low to the ground. Though small, Dachshunds are not frail.

Breed Profile: The Dachshund is a sassy, playful, spirited breed that acts like a terrier. It has a superior scenting ability and may be stubborn, dominant, and somewhat resistant to training. Nevertheless, the Dachshund is very personable and can make a great companion.

A difference in temperament exists not between the two sizes but among the three coat varieties. The smooth is usually alert, bold, and friendly. The longhaired is usually more timid and reserved with strangers and requires a more patient training technique. The wirehaired tends to be the most active of the three and, though friendly, is the most stubborn.

The Dachshund requires firm consistent obedience training and early socialization. Its great sense of smell will often lead it astray, so make sure you develop a no-nonsense training attitude. The Come command can be difficult to teach to this breed. If spoiled, which is often the case, this breed may get snappy, so don't pamper your Dachshund. It may be small, but it is very pushy and will take over if given the chance. This breed can be a barker and will make a good watchdog.

Handle your Dachshund puppy often. It must learn that you have a right to clean its ears, trim its toenails, brush it, and inspect its body.

Housebreaking can be difficult, particularly with the miniature.

Don't let your Dachshund get overweight. Its long back and short legs will not easily support extra bulk. Also, keep its nails trimmed to prevent distortion of the foot placement, which can cause arthritis later in life.

The Dachshund, especially the smooth version, can be susceptible to cold weather. Provide it with a sweater.

Best Home: An apartment is fine as long as the dog is exercised daily. Bear in mind that this breed can bark loudly. The owner of a Dachshund should be a consistent, patient leader who desires a small, active, personable breed. Children are okay provided they are considerate and are not allowed to roughhouse with the dog. The Dachshund requires firm training and socialization from the start, so make sure you have the time. Also, you will need to work hard on the Come command.

Don't spoil your Dachshund. Spoiled dogs think they are in charge, and they think it's acceptable to bite. And don't let it sleep in bed with you! This undermines your authority and is the quickest road to a biting Dachshund.

The elderly and the disabled can own this breed provided they are able to train and exercise it.

Foxhound, American

Origins: Imported from France and England in the seventeenth and eighteenth century, this scent hound was used in packs or singly for fox hunts. It is now used as a competitive field trial dog.

Appearance: The American Foxhound stands 21 to 25 inches at the shoulder and weighs between 55 and 75 pounds. It has a large, strong, athletic body and a short, dense, shedding coat that is stiff to the touch. It requires only periodic brushing. The coat is black, white, and tan.

Breed Profile: Larger than the English Foxhound, the American is a hunting breed first and foremost. It doesn't make a great house pet and will drive you nuts because of its high energy level. It can be very stubborn and is easily distracted by scent. It is happiest when tracking, hunting, or doing some other type of field work.

The American Foxhound is suspicious of strangers and makes a good watchdog, but it can be dog-aggressive.

The American Foxhound will be good-natured with your children, but it may knock them down and hurt them while playing.

Though distractable, the American Foxhound does not normally exhibit the type of non-thinking aggression common to Bloodhounds and Coonhounds. It is very noisy, however, and if left alone, can be restless and destructive.

Training and socialization should begin early. As with all hounds, the Come command is hard to perfect.

Best Home: A hunter or a very active person should own this breed. A house in the country with a fenced yard or kennel is essential. Children are fine as long as no roughhousing is allowed. Plenty of directed exercise is needed to avoid restlessness, barking, and digging. The owner must be a firm no-nonsense leader who has time to train, socialize, and exercise the dog. This is not a lapdog and won't do well with an easygoing, elderly, or disabled owner.

Foxhound, English

Origins: The English Foxhound, which dates back to sixteenth- and seventeenth-century England, is still used in packs for fox hunts. This dog's genealogy has remained relatively pure for hundreds of years.

Appearance: The English Foxhound stands 20 to 24 inches at the shoulder and weighs between 50 and 65 pounds. It has a strong, athletic, medium to large body that is slightly smaller than that of the American Foxhound. The short, dense, shedding coat is low maintenance, requiring only periodic brushing. The coat is black, white, and tan.

Breed Profile: Though smaller than the American Foxhound, the English has the same basic temperament. It is a hunter by nature and has a high energy level that makes it difficult to own as a family house pet. It needs a job, specifically hunting.

Though suspicious of strangers and potentially dog-aggressive, this breed will not show the non-thinking aggression that is sometimes seen in Bloodhounds and Coonhounds. English Foxhounds love children, but because of their energy and strength, they must be carefully watched around toddlers. They need a great deal of exercise and will become restless and destructive without it. All Foxhounds are easily distracted by their powerful sense of smell; this is a major impediment to obedience training.

The English Foxhound is noisy and makes an excellent watch dog. Obedience training must begin early; the Come command is the hardest to teach because of scent distraction.

Best Home: An English Foxhound will do best with a very active owner, preferably a hunter. A rural environment with a fenced yard or kennel is essential. Firm, no-nonsense leadership is required, as is regular exercise, to avoid restlessness and destructive behavior. The elderly and the disabled should not own this breed. Children are fine as long as no roughhousing is allowed.

Greyhound

Origins: One of the oldest breeds, this sight hound was used by the Egyptians to run down rabbits and gazelles on the open plains of northern Africa. The Greyhound is currently, and unfortunately, used as a racing dog, and is often destroyed after a short, impersonal career.

Appearance: Greyhounds are large, sleek dogs, standing 26 to 28 inches at the shoulder and weighing 60 to 70 pounds. Lean and agile, they were bred as desert hunters, and they have virtually no body fat. This allows them to tolerate heat well, but it makes them a poor choice for cold climates. Their coat is a short, shedding type, requiring minimal maintenance. Colors include white, brindle, gray, and tan, among others.

Breed Profile: The Greyhound is a sweet, sensitive dog that can be aloof with strangers if not socialized properly from an early age. Normally quiet, it can be a good apartment pet if exercised regularly. It likes to curl up on a dog bed or sheepskin and be lazy most of the day. Though affectionate, it does not have the ''pet me, love me, touch me'' attitude of a Lab or a Golden.

Greyhounds learn rather slowly. You must be patient and take things in small steps so as not to confuse them. The Sit command is hard for them to master. Do not use the bold training methods with a Greyhound that you might use with a Mastiff or a Rottweiler, or the dog may panic and possibly bite or run. Be patient and positive. Confidence-building is important in the training of a Greyhound.

The Greyhound can be aggressive toward small dogs, and it has a high prey drive toward cats, rabbits, and other small animals.

Most sight hounds have little padding on their bodies and can get pressure sores if they're not provided with something soft to lie on. The Greyhound is no exception. It will not do well in an outdoor kennel, particularly in a cold climate; it must be kept warm or it may get sick. It won't tolerate playful roughhousing the way a retriever would, but the Greyhound can make a great jogging partner and is normally very well behaved on leash. If you like a sweet, quiet, sensitive dog that will love you and yet be content to amuse itself, then a Greyhound might be a good choice.

Recently we have helped to retrain Greyhounds that were rescued from numerous racetracks around the country. Dog racing is a miserable, morbid business; the dogs race until they are two or three years of age, whereupon many of them are destroyed. A number of rescue groups have begun taking these animals in and finding good homes for them. If you choose to take one of these Greyhounds, remember that these dogs need time to get used to living in a household. They have never been house-trained because they have lived in pens from birth, and they may be a bit skittish as well. Still, we have had great luck in helping them adapt to normal living.

Best Home: A quiet, predictable home with no young children is the best environment for a Greyhound. It can live in an apartment if it's exercised daily. The owner should be calm and confident, and not use overbearing training methods. Nervous, cautious types will serve only to worry this sensitive breed. The owner must be a patient leader, as the Greyhound takes longer to train than other breeds. Small animals in the home may be a problem due to the breed's strong prey drive.

The Greyhound owner should not be a person who needs a clingy, overly affectionate dog. Though sweet, this breed needs its space.

Harrier

Origins: The beginnings of this breed are unclear, though there is some evidence that it existed in medieval England, and perhaps even earlier on the European continent. It was bred to hunt foxes and rabbits and has traditionally been used in packs.

Appearance: The Harrier stands 19 to 21 inches at the shoulder and weighs between 40 and 55 pounds. It has a strong, athletic body similar to that of the English and American Foxhounds, but smaller. The shedding coat is short, stiff, and of very low maintenance. The color is a combination of black, white, and tan.

Breed Profile: This hunting breed has a high energy level that makes it a difficult house pet. It needs to hunt.

Though initially suspicious of strangers, the Harrier does not have the potential for non-thinking aggression that is sometimes seen in Bloodhounds and Coonhounds. It is typically good with the family, but may need to be watched with small children, who could be knocked down and injured.

This breed is easily distracted by scent; this can present a major challenge in training. Obedience training should start early; the Come command is the toughest for this breed to learn. The Harrier needs a great deal of exercise and will become restless and destructive without it. If left in a yard, it may bark and dig.

Best Home: A Harrier should be owned by an active person, preferably a hunter. A rural environment with a fenced yard or kennel is essential. Firm leadership and regular exercise are required. The elderly and the disabled may have trouble with the energy level of this athletic breed. Older children are fine as long as no roughhousing is permitted.

Ibizan Hound

Origins: This ancient breed found favor among the Egyptians, Phoenicians, and Romans for its ability to locate rabbits and other small game animals by sight and then to run them down.

Appearance: The Ibizan Hound stands 22.5 to 27.5 inches at the shoulder and weighs 40 to 50 pounds. It has a lithe, athletic body with a short, shedding, low-maintenance coat. The coat may also be wirehaired, but this is equally low maintenance. The color may be red or tan with white on the chest, forehead, and legs.

Breed Profile: This lithe, active sight hound has a reserved, dignified, quiet demeanor, and is not comfortable in a hectic environment. Though affectionate with its owners, it does not need or desire constant attention. The Ibizan Hound is friendlier than a Saluki or a Borzoi, however, having a temperament more akin to that of the Whippet.

The Ibizan Hound is a slow learner; training must proceed slowly and with great precision. Let the dog know exactly what you want of it, and take it in small steps. Overbearing methods will panic this breed.

The Ibizan can be dog-aggressive and has a high prey drive toward small animals. It does better in homes without smaller children. Obedience training, socialization, and handling should all begin early in the dog's life. The Come command is the most important one for a sight hound to know.

Best Home: An apartment will do if the dog receives daily exercise. A quiet, predictable home without young children is the best environment for this breed. The owner of an Ibizan should be a calm, confident, patient leader who has time to socialize the dog. Nervous and overbearing persons should avoid this breed. Small animals in the home may pose a problem due to this breed's high prey drive.

Irish Wolfhound

Origins: This tallest of all breeds was used in medieval Ireland as a hunter of wolf and elk and may have existed as far back as Roman times. Though considered a sight hound, the Irish Wolfhound was bred to have excellent scenting ability as well.

Appearance: The Irish Wolfhound stands 30 to 34 inches at the shoulder and weighs between 100 and 125 pounds. It has a statuesque, muscular body and a rough, weather-resistant shedding coat that requires only periodic brushing. The color may be gray, fawn, brindle, red, white, or black.

Breed Profile: This giant tends to be somewhat more gregarious than the Borzoi and Afghan. Gentle and often on the timid side, it needs at least two years to mature physically and emotionally. Like the other sight hounds, this breed is quiet and calm in the home, but because of its sheer size it requires a house with a large fenced yard. Be aware that this breed can easily jump a six-foot fence.

The Irish Wolfhound learns slowly. Use patience, and expect the training to take a bit longer than it would with other breeds. A positive attitude and lots of confidence-building are needed. Overbearing training methods will panic this sensitive giant. Be patient and precise.

Though usually friendly, this breed, given its great size, could easily hurt a child while playing. Initially suspicious of strangers, the Irish Wolfhound can also be aggressive toward dogs and small animals. Socialization, training, and handling must begin early.

Irish Wolfhounds can be susceptible to bloat and hip dysplasia, and on average live only eight to ten years. Also, bear in mind that food will be a great expense with this breed. To help prevent bloat, a life-threatening gaseous torsion of the stomach, break up feedings into smaller portions, and soak the food in warm water for ten minutes before feeding.

Best Home: A quiet, predictable home with a fenced yard and no young children is best. The owner must be a patient, calm leader with no overbearing tendencies. This is not the breed for someone who wants to prove his or her machismo. Regular exercise must be provided, along with training, socialization, and handling. The owner must have time available for this. The elderly and the disabled should avoid this breed because of its great size, as should those who desire the gregariousness of a Lab or a Golden. The owner must also be able to afford the large quantities of food this breed will consume.

Norwegian Elkhound

Origins: Used as a herd guarder and a hunter of elk and other game, this venerable breed traces its lineage back to Viking days. It was bred to have strength, an excellent sense of smell, endurance, and stamina in the cold Norwegian winter.

Appearance: The Norwegian Elkhound stands 19 to 21 inches at the shoulder and weighs between 45 to 60 pounds. It has a robust, well-muscled body and a medium-length, thick, insulating coat with a dense undercoat. Shedding is year-round, and the dog requires daily brushing. The color is silver-and-gray with black-tipped guard hairs dispersed throughout the coat.

Breed Profile: The Norwegian Elkhound exhibits intelligence, strength, and alertness. Its sense of smell is strong and will serve to distract the dog. Independent, dominant, and stubborn, this breed can be a challenge to train. One must be firm and consistent to gain leadership over a Norwegian Elkhound.

Initially suspicious of strangers, the Elkhound makes a good watchdog, but it must receive socialization from an early age in order to modify its tendency toward territorial aggression. It can be aggressive toward other dogs and small animals. Bred to bark upon locating prey, the Elkhound has retained this habit, which, combined with its energy and athleticism, makes it an unlikely apartment dog.

We don't recommend this breed for those who have small children, and roughhousing and tug-of-war must not be permitted. Training must begin early and must focus particularly on the Come command.

Best Home: A house with a fenced yard is essential, as is daily exercise. Older children are okay, providing there is no roughhousing. The owner of a Norwegian Elkhound must be a strong leader, and must be able to establish and maintain the dominant position. Spoilers will create a dominant, pushy, potentially aggressive dog. Owners must allot time for daily training, grooming, and exercise. Weak leaders, cautious or nervous types, and those concerned about shedding should pass on this breed. Consider a female rather than a male; they often make better, more controllable house pets. We also advise the elderly and the disabled against choosing this restive breed.

Otterhound

Origins: Used in medieval England to hunt down otters that were depleting the local fish population, this large scent hound was bred to love water.

Appearance: The Otterhound stands 23 to 27 inches at the shoulder and weighs between 75 and 110 pounds. It has a large, powerful body and head, and webbed feet to aid in swimming. The outer coat is rough and weather-resistant, and is of medium length and maintenance. The undercoat is soft and oily in texture, acting as insulation against cold river water. The color may be black-and-tan, gray, or white with blue shadings.

Breed Profile: Now more of a companion than a hunting dog, this breed still retains the drive and instincts of a hunter and can be used as such. Active and strong, the Otterhound has the stubborn streak so typical of scent hounds. Training must begin early and must be firm and consistent. Though friendly to its family, the Otterhound can be suspicious of strangers, necessitating early socialization. Exercise, particularly swimming, is essential; without it, an Otterhound may become restless, noisy, and destructive.

Because of its rambunctious nature, this large dog is not recommended for families with small children, who might get knocked down and hurt during play. No roughhousing or tug-of-war should be tolerated.

Like all large breeds, the Otterhound is susceptible to hip dysplasia and bloat.

Best Home: A house with a fenced yard is essential for this large, energetic scent hound, as is regular exercise, preferably swimming.

This is a high-powered breed that will not suit you if you are looking for a thoughtful, easygoing pet. The Otterhound needs some job or directed task to perform, preferably hunting, tracking, or agility work.

Firm, no-nonsense leadership is essential, as are early obedience training and socialization. The owner of this breed should be confident and dominant. Submissive, cautious, nervous, or spoiling types should avoid this breed, as should the elderly and the disabled. Older children are all right as long as no roughhousing occurs, but take care when your children have friends over.

Petit Basset Griffon Vendéen

Origins: Used in Western France as far back as the sixteenth century to track rabbits, this low-slung breed could penetrate brush that was impenetrable to larger breeds. Its excellent sense of smell, hardy physique, and weather-resistant coat made it perfectly suited to its original purpose.

Appearance: The Petit Basset Griffon Vendén, or PBGV, stands 13 to 15 inches at the shoulder and weighs between 35 and 45 pounds. Its body is sturdy, athletic, and strong. The shedding outer coat is rough and wiry, and the undercoat is thick and short. It requires a daily brushing, and an occasional trim. The PBGV's ears are long and covered with long hair. The colors are white with lemon, orange, grizzle, or black markings.

Breed Profile: Alert, bold and playful, the PBGV is a friendly, stubborn scent hound with an independent, busy attitude. It can be difficult to train because of its distracting sense of smell and its rambunctious nature. It is similar to the Basset Hound in temperament, albeit somewhat more active.

This breed can be a good family dog if trained early and given plenty of exercise. Though small, the PBGV doesn't do well in an apartment due to its activity level and its penchant for barking. It can be susceptible to ear infections and may need regular ear cleanings.

Best Home: A house with a fenced yard is preferable. The owner of a PBGV should be an active leader who desires a busy, energetic dog. Submissive, pampering types and those who want a quiet, lazy pet should avoid this breed. The elderly and the disabled can own a PBGV provided they are able to train and exercise it. Older children are okay, providing no roughhousing occurs. Early obedience training and daily exercise are necessary to direct this rambunctious breed's impetuous nature.

Pharaoh Hound

Origins: An ancient breed, this medium-size sight hound was used by Egyptian nobility to hunt rabbits and gazelles.

Appearance: The Pharaoh Hound stands 21 to 25 inches at the shoulder and weighs between 45 and 60 pounds. It has a lithe, athletic, graceful body and a short, glossy, shedding coat that is very easy to maintain. The color may be tan or red. The Pharaoh Hound has amber eyes similar in color to those of the Weimaraner.

Breed Profile: The Pharaoh Hound, though typically reserved, is not as cautious with strangers as the Greyhound or Saluki. It is quiet, clean, and easygoing in the home. Though tolerant of older children, it will not appreciate a hectic environment or any kind of roughhousing. The Pharaoh Hound will not make a good watchdog and must be watched around small animals because of its high prey drive. Like all sight hounds, the Pharaoh Hound, though well behaved indoors, needs daily exercise to remain happy and healthy.

Training can take longer than normal with this breed. No rushed or overbearing techniques should be used. Patience and precision are needed because of the slow speed at which all sight hounds learn. If pushed, the dog may panic and become passive-resistant, taking a "head in the sand" attitude. The Sit and Come commands are the most challenging to teach. Early socialization will help reduce this breed's natural timidity.

Best Home: The Pharaoh Hound can live in an apartment if the dog is exercised daily. Keep in mind that this breed can jump a six-foot fence. The environment should be quiet, predictable, and free of hectic activity. The Pharaoh Hound will not tolerate roughhousing and may snap in protest.

The owner of a Pharaoh Hound should be easygoing and respectful of this breed's need for space. Provide a place for the dog to call its own, perhaps a sheepskin or a bed in the corner of the living room. Those who want an affectionate hands-on pet should consider a retriever, not a sight hound. Overbearing, loud people should avoid this breed. Most sight hounds do not do well with small pets, particularly rabbits or rodents, so avoid the temptation.

Rhodesian Ridgeback

Origins: Developed in South Africa in the eighteenth century, the Rhodesian Ridgeback filled the need for a strong dog that could hunt big game over vast areas in extreme temperatures. This dog could go for long periods without water and, with the help of its excellent vision and sense of smell, could detect the approach of camp marauders, either animal or human.

It is thought that Great Danes, Mastiffs, Bloodhounds, and perhaps Greyhounds were interbred to produce this breed.

Appearance: The Rhodesian Ridgeback stands 24 to 27 inches at the shoulder and weighs between 65 and 85 pounds. It has a large, powerful, well-muscled body and a short, stiff, shedding coat with a characteristic ridge of hair on its back that grows in the opposite direction and seems to have no function. The coat requires only periodic brushing. The color is always a reddish brown, sometimes with white patches on the chest and feet.

Breed Profile: The Rhodesian Ridgeback has some characteristics of both a sight hound and scent hound. It is independent, active, often dominant and stubbornly driven, and yet curiously sensitive like a Greyhound. Affectionate yet pushy with its owner, the Rhodesian Ridgeback may be suspicious of strangers. Its excellent sense of smell acts as a great distraction in this breed's life and makes training difficult, but the Ridgeback is an excellent watchdog.

This is a strong breed that needs obedience training from day one. The method must be firm but not overbearing, as the dog may panic and become passive-resistant if pressed too hard. Slow, precise methods are called for. Socialization with people is essential, too, as this breed can be aggressive if threatened. Remember also that the Rhodesian Ridgeback was bred to challenge lions, leopards, and hyenas, and may therefore be dog-aggressive if not socialized with other dogs from early on. As with all breeds, neutering the males will help reduce this problem especially if it is done before eight months of age. The females tend to be much more sensitive than the males and should be trained with a less demanding technique.

Because of the Ridgeback's great size and power, we advise against choosing this breed if small children are present. Certainly no roughhousing should occur. Do not leave this breed alone for long periods. It may be noisy and destructive, and it can jump a fence.

Do not be tempted to buy two Rhodesian Ridgebacks from the same litter. One is a handful. Two, particularly from the same litter, may be draining and potentially dangerous. Littermates tend to bond closely with each other and will often openly disobey the owner in favor of pack loyalties.

Best Home: A house with a yard is essential, but don't leave the dog there constantly; you may create a destructive, noisy dog. The owner of a Rhodesian Ridgeback must be a firm leader who is consistent and patient. Pampering or spoiling may create an obnoxious, pushy dog that lacks confidence—all the ingredients for major problems. Nervous, submissive, placating, and overbearing people should avoid this breed, as should those with young or rambunctious children. The elderly and the disabled should also look elsewhere.

Regular exercise is mandatory. Joggers do well with this breed, which has tremendous endurance. Those who live in extremely cold climates should avoid this breed.

Saluki

Origins: The Saluki may very well be the oldest domesticated breed. The Egyptians, Mesopotamians, and Persians all have records of Saluki-type dogs used by the nobility as coursing hounds in hunting rabbits and small gazelles. The Saluki was bred for speed and agility and has remarkable vision.

Appearance: The Saluki stands 23 to 28 inches at the shoulder and weighs between 40 and 60 pounds. It has a lean, supple body, and a short, silky, shedding coat that is feathered on the legs, thighs, tail, and ears and needs to be brushed two or three times a week. The color may be white, cream, tricolor (black, white, and tan), fawn, beige or red.

Breed Profile: The Saluki is the archetypal sight hound, both behaviorally and physically. It is fast, agile, and has excellent vision. It is aloof and reserved with strangers, preferring not to interact with those outside its pack. Strangers should be advised not to pet a Saluki without giving the dog time to get accustomed to them.

Training can be difficult. The Saluki is somewhat stubborn and does not process information quickly. The training technique must therefore be slow and precise, with no overbearing methods. If you push too hard or too fast a Saluki will stop thinking and become passive-resistant, taking a head-in-the-sand attitude, or becoming snappy.

The Saluki is a clean, quiet dog that prefers a predictable, quiet environment with a space to call its own. Too much hectic activity may stress it out. This breed is not recommended for families with young children. Though affectionate with its owners, don't expect a Saluki to be as loving and desirous of touch as a Lab or a Spaniel. It exudes an almost feline air. If you prefer a clean, quiet dog that is not always at your feet begging for attention, then this might be it.

Best Home: An apartment will do if the dog is exercised regularly. A daily run is recommended. The owner of a Saluki should be an easygoing leader who is not seeking an extremely active, social dog, and who instead prefers a dog that is content to curl up on a sheepskin and get lost in its own thoughts. Overbearing, impatient persons should avoid this breed, as should pampering types and those with young children. The elderly and the disabled will need to be able to exercise a Saluki if they are to own one.

The owner of a Saluki must find time to train and socialize the dog as often as possible early on so as to modify its aloof, suspicious nature.

Scottish Deerhound

Origins: Although known primarily as a Scottish breed, Deerhound-type dogs have been around since ancient times. First used by Scottish hunters to chase and bring down large deer, this breed has a rough coat that protects it from the cold. Though it is known as a sight hound, its sense of smell is also acute.

Appearance: The Scottish Deerhound stands 30 to 32 inches at the shoulder and weighs between 75 and 110 pounds. It has a lean, athletic, lanky body that is similar to but thinner and slightly shorter than that of the Irish Wolfhound. The Deerhound's shedding coat is rough and wiry and of medium length. It requires periodic brushing and an occasional trim. The color may be blue-gray, fawn, light gray, or brindle.

Breed Profile: This beautiful, elegant dignified breed is typically quiet, gentle, and reserved with strangers. Though lazy and easygoing in the home, it does need a daily run to stay happy and healthy.

The Scottish Deerhound prefers a quiet, predictable environment and does not easily tolerate the hectic activity of young children. It may also be dog-aggressive, and it has a high prey drive toward small animals. This breed needs obedience training and socialization from an early age to combat its timidity and increase its confidence. If scared or annoyed, a Deerhound may bite. Training must be slow and precise, for this breed learns slowly. Overbearing methods may cause it to panic or become passive-resistant, a condition in which a dog stops thinking and seems frozen. Patience and consistency are required. The Sit and Come commands may be the hardest to teach to a Deerhound.

The Scottish Deerhound usually lives only ten to twelve years and can suffer from bloat, or torsion of the stomach, an often fatal condition. To help avoid this, break the dog's feedings down into at least two a day, and soak the dry food in warm water for five minutes before feeding. This will minimize the chance of swelling and of gaseous buildup in the stomach, a leading contributor to bloat.

Best Home: Because of the Deerhound's great size, we recommend a house with a fenced yard—bear in mind that these dogs can jump a six-foot fence. The owner of this breed should be patient and easygoing, never harsh, loud, or hyperactive. Pampering types should also pass, as should those who are looking for an extremely gregarious, playful dog. Deerhounds are not recommended for families with young children. The elderly and disabled might have trouble providing this breed with enough exercise.

Time to train and socialize is imperative, as is a daily run. A jogger might enjoy this dog. A blanket or bed should be provided for this breed to lie on because of the lack of fat and muscle padding on its frame. Above all, allow this breed its own space, socialize it, and don't expect it to act like a Lab or a Golden Retriever.

Whippet

Origins: A relatively new breed, the Whippet first appeared in the nineteenth century in England. A cross between the Greyhound and perhaps the Smooth Fox Terrier, the Whippet has been used for rabbit coursing, ratting, and racing.

Appearance: The Whippet stands 18 to 22 inches at the shoulder and weighs between 18 and 35 pounds. It has a lean, athletic body and a short, smooth, low-maintenance shedding coat that requires only a quick weekly brushing. The color can be white, black, tan, brindle, or pinto.

Breed Profile: Though one of the friendlist of the sight hounds, the Whippet can be initially nervous and reserved around strangers. Playful and affectionate with its owners, the Whippet will appreciate a good run once per day.

The Whippet is clean and quiet and makes an excellent apartment dog, preferring to spend much of the day curled up on a blanket or bed in the corner of the living room. Make sure you respect its desire and need to be in its own space every now and then.

Obedience training should start early and should include as much socialization as possible to limit this breed's timid tendencies. Training technique should be positive, patient, and precise, for the Whippet, like other sight hounds, learns slowly and will stop thinking if given too much information to process at one time. Never use harsh methods on this sensitive breed. The Sit and Come commands may be the most difficult to teach to a Whippet.

The Whippet will probably be tolerant of older children, as long as the children do not roughhouse or create a hectic, unpredictable environment. This breed should be watched around small animals, particularly rabbits. Whippets are susceptible to cold weather and do better in arid climates.

Don't leave a Whippet in the yard all day. It can jump fences quite well and will do so if bored or restless.

Best Home: An apartment is acceptable, provided the dog is exercised daily. A quiet place should always be available to a Whippet when it needs to get away from hectic activity. This breed is not recommended for families with young children.

The owner of a Whippet should be a patient, easygoing leader who will appreciate a dog that enjoys affection but does not demand it. Nervous, hyperactive, or overbearing persons may stress this breed out. The elderly and the disabled should do well with this breed, if they are able to exercise it. The owner must have time to train and socialize this breed.

Section Four

The Working Group

Breeds in the Working Group include the mastiff types, the herd guarders, and the northern breeds, known for pulling sleds. Rottweilers, Great Pyrenees, and Malamutes are all contained here. Most of the working breeds are large, dominant, strong dogs with courage and stamina. Most are very territorial and require a confident owner with great leadership skills.

Akita

Origins: Named after a prefecture on the island of Honshu, Japan, this breed was initially developed as a versatile hunting dog with power, size, a good sense of smell, insulation against the cold, and a dominant, aggressive nature that enabled it to deal with bears, deer, and wild boars. Over the centuries the Akita came to be  revered as a noble breed and a spiritual symbol of loyalty and beauty.

Appearance: The Akita stands 24 to 28 inches at the shoulder and weighs between 80 and 110 pounds. It is thick-boned and has a large, powerful body. The harsh, shedding coat is of medium length with a thick, dense undercoat. This breed sheds year-round and requires frequent brushing. Colors include white, brindle, white with tan patches, and other combinations.

Breed Profile: This is a strong, athletic, personable breed that, though affectionate, can be quite stubborn and controlling if its owner does not establish dominance early on. Although the Akita is usually easygoing in the home, it may exhibit marked territorial instincts, showing a reserved, suspicious nature with strangers. This dog is normally affectionate toward family members, but it will constantly vie for the dominant position and will use its body and mouth to exert control over those in the family who have not yet established dominance. Aggression toward family members is common when leadership is not established. No one should ever be permitted to roughhouse with this breed.

The Akita can be very dog-aggressive and has a high prey drive toward small animals. It may not do well with small children, seeing them as subordinate littermates who may need disciplining from time to time.

Obedience training, socialization, and handling must start early with this breed and must be firm, precise, and slow, as the Akita doesn't learn quickly and can become confused. This breed is very stubborn and may occasionally throw a tantrum when resisting. The Akita is one of the more difficult breeds to train.

The Akita bitch, though just as pushy as the male, tends to be a worrier when young. Both sexes are susceptible to urinary tract infections when young and are hard to housebreak. They can also be prone to hip dysplasia.

If you decide on a male, have him neutered by the seventh or eighth month. This will make training easier, will reduce aggression and dominance problems, and can prevent marking in the house.

People often buy Akita littermates. *Don't do this.* They will bond more closely to each other than to you, making control a major issue. They will also exhibit more territorial aggression. Never get littermates of any breed, especially dogs of a dominant breed such as this.

The Akita, with its thick, insulating coat, loves cold weather and likes to play in the snow. Don't get one if you live in a warm climate. Avoid jogging with this breed, as it is big-boned and heavy and might develop arthritis later in life.

Best Home: A house with a fenced yard is essential, as is daily exercise. The owner of an Akita must be a natural leader and should desire an affectionate, independent dog that will be a challenge. Overbearing, submissive, nervous, and cautious people should avoid this breed, as should those with small children. The owner must be up to the physical challenge as well, as these dogs are very large and powerful. Because of this we recommend that the elderly, the diminutive, and the disabled pass on this breed.

The owner of an Akita must find the time to train, socialize, handle, and groom it and must not keep it exclusively in the yard, where it will become noisy, territorial, and destructive.

Alaskan Malamute

Origins: Named after the Mahlemuts, an Inuit tribe of northwestern Alaska, this giant Arctic breed has been used as a sled dog. Bred for strength, endurance, and independence, it has the ability to tolerate extremely low temperatures. Today Malamutes are used in sled-pulling competitions, some being able to pull a sled weighing close to a ton.

Appearance: The Alaskan Malamute stands 23 to 26 inches at the shoulder and usually weighs 75 to 125 pounds, though some are even larger. It is thick-boned and has a large, muscular body. The weather-resistant coat is thick, heavy, and of medium length. The undercoat is dense and insulative. Malamutes shed copiously year-round, particularly in early summer. This breed requires frequent brushing. The color may be black-and-white with an off-white undercoat, red-and-white, or gray-and-white with an off-white undercoat.

Breed Profile: This friendly, oafish, powerful breed is good-natured but stubborn. Usually good with children and friends, the Malamute doesn't make a good watchdog, but it does have a high prey drive and will show aggression toward other dogs. It can be impetuous, dominant, and challenging, and is not the most cooperative breed with regard to obedience training. Early training is essential due to the breed's size, level of dominance, and aggression toward animals. The Come command is the most difficult to teach a Malamute because of its independent, free-thinking nature, though the females tend to be less dominant and aggressive, and roam less. A firm, consistent training technique must be used with this sometimes resistant breed. Never baby or spoil this dominant breed in any way.

The Malamute tends to be quite vocal, and can be very destructive if not exercised daily. Though these dogs are friendly, care must be taken to see that this large breed does not knock over and hurt a child. No roughhousing or chase games should be tolerated.

The Malamute loves to dig, and will create crater-sized holes all over your yard. Building a large kennel with a concrete floor will eliminate this problem. This breed can be left outside during even the coldest winter. It won't phase them at all.

Although Malamutes are almost always good-natured, we have seen a few cases of aggression toward people with this breed, particularly from the males. Tremendously strong and determined, a Malamute can do serious damage in a matter of moments. Once this behavior occurs, it is very difficult to modify and usually results in the destruction of the animal.

The Malamute lives for only ten to twelve years and can suffer from hip dysplasia, shoulder problems, and bloat. It loves the cold and will suffer in warmer climates. It needs exercise, but should not be run long distances due to its weight and susceptibility to hip and shoulder problems. This breed eats large amounts of food (an expense to consider) and can develop diarrhea if the diet is changed too rapidly. Altering can lengthen a Malamute's life and help prevent aggression and a host of other behavioral problems.

Best Home: A house with a fenced yard or kennel is essential for this big, independent breed. It needs a firm, consistent, nononsense leader who is confident and physically able to deal with such a powerful, impetuous breed. Older children can be okay if absolutely no roughhousing or chasing is allowed. Training should begin early and should include daily socialization, handling, and grooming. We do not recommend any small pets in the household. Diminutive, spoiling, cautious, and overbearing persons should avoid this breed, as should the elderly and the disabled.

Bernese Mountain Dog

Origins: An old breed of Swiss origin, the Bernese Mountain Dog was bred for herd-guarding, drafting, and droving. Its large, sturdy frame and long coat allowed it to perform in cold mountainous environments.

Appearance: The Bernese Mountain Dog stands 23 to 27.5 inches at the shoulder and weighs between 70 and 100 pounds. It is a large breed and is similar to the Golden Retriever in structure, only heavier and bigger-boned. The shedding coat is medium-long, wavy, glossy, and thick and requires regular brushing. The Bernese is tricolored—primarily black with rust and white markings on the chest, muzzle, feet, and forehead.

Breed Profile: This large, athletic breed, though playful and gregarious as a pup, tends to become more reserved and guarded as it matures. Though normally affectionate to its owner, the Bernese can be very suspicious of strangers. We have worked with some that were timid to the point of being phobic. This potential for extreme shyness can lead to a fear-based aggression that is difficult to modify. Complicating the issue is this breed's normally dominant, headstrong temperament. Stubbornness normally calls for a firm, consistent training technique, but many Bernese, particularly the females, can slip into a panicky mind-set if pushed, sometimes resulting in a bite. We believe this phobic tendency to be a result of poor breeding practices, and may not be reversible. When this phobic tendency is absent, the Bernese Mountain Dog is trainable, but patience and precision are crucial.

The Bernese needs daily exercise and is happier in a rural environment. We do not presently recommend this breed for families with children because of the potential for aggression. Early socialization is important, as are handling and grooming.

The Bernese Mountain Dog lives only ten to twelve years and can suffer from hip dysplasia and bloat. Anyone interested in this breed should visit numerous breeders and closely observe the parents and littermates. Attempt to observe both parents before you choose a puppy.

Best Home: A house with a fenced yard is essential. A strong, patient leader with patience is mandatory, as are early training, handling, and socialization. Families with children should at present avoid this breed, as should nervous, cautious, placating and overbearing people. The elderly and the disabled may not be able to handle this large, active breed.

Boxer

Origins: Perfected in Germany during the nineteenth century, this active breed was developed by crossing Mastiff, Bulldog, and terrier bloodlines and was once used for fighting and bullbaiting. Today's Boxers, however, do not have the fierce temperament of the earlier dogs.

Appearance: The Boxer stands 21 to 25 inches at the shoulder and weighs 55 to 75 pounds. Strong and thickly muscled, it has a short muzzle, a docked tail, and cropped or uncropped ears. The shedding coat is short, stiff, somewhat prickly to the touch, and of very low maintenance, requiring only an occasional brushing. The color may be brindle with white or fawn with white.

Breed Profile: This is a friendly, headstrong, high-energy breed that is very affectionate but easily distracted. A busy, curious breed, the Boxer needs firm, precise obedience training from an early age in order to contain its boundless energy, but the training should not be overbearing or rushed. The Boxer can be suspicious of strangers and, in some cases, may be dog- or people-aggressive, especially the male. Daily exercise is mandatory; this dog makes an excellent jogging partner and agility dog.

The Boxer is normally good with children, but care must be taken that this strong breed does not knock down and hurt a child. Roughhousing, wrestling, and chasing should be forbidden.

The Boxer has little cushioning on its body and needs a blanket or bed to lie on. It has no body fat and therefore gets cold easily and does not do well in northern climates. It is also prone to respiratory problems, is a horrendous snorer and sneezer, and can be flatulent. The Boxer is susceptible to heart problems and bloat and normally lives only ten to twelve years.

Best Home: A house with a fenced yard is essential. The owner of a Boxer should be an active, strong, competent leader who has the time and patience to work, socialize, and exercise this energetic, often stubborn breed. Children are okay provided no roughhousing occurs. Persons who are very easygoing or slow-moving should avoid this breed, as should those who are nervous, cautious, overbearing, or meek. Placating people will have a hard time controlling this breed and may create a dominant dog that lacks confidence. The elderly and the disabled should avoid this powerful, busy breed.

Bullmastiff

Origins: Though the Mastiff is an ancient breed, the Bullmastiff was not developed until fairly recently, in nineteenth-century England. A cross between the Mastiff and the Bulldog, it filled the need for a dog to challenge and capture poachers who were hunting on large estates. The Bullmastiff was bred to be courageous, quick, strong, and willing to challenge humans.

Appearance: The Bullmastiff stands 24 to 27 inches at the shoulder and weighs between 100 and 135 pounds. It has a powerful, heavily muscled and boned body and a short, low-maintenance shedding coat. Ears are cropped or uncropped. The color may be fawn, reddish brown, or brindle; a small white patch on the chest is acceptable.

Breed Profile: The Bullmastiff is an affectionate, lazy, powerful breed that is a natural guardian of home and family. These dogs are usually very suspicious of strangers and other dogs and are one of the most territorial of breeds. Though normally gentle with children in their own family, Bullmastiff's can be unpredictable with friends, relatives, and co-workers. It must be understood that this breed was designed to challenge human beings and will do so without hesitation if a threat is perceived. When a Bullmastiff becomes aggressive, it is explosive and unstoppable. This breed is capable of killing another dog in seconds, so do not consider letting it off leash. The only way to minimize this instinctive behavior is to socialize and train the dog from the first day, allowing the Bullmastiff puppy to interact with people and dogs in a controlled, positive environment. Males should be neutered by the eighth month. Females tend to be less aggressive and a bit more timid than males.

The Bullmastiff is normally content to lie around the house. Though less energetic than the Boxer, it does tend to be slightly more active than the Mastiff.

Training should begin early and should be firm but not overbearing, as this breed matures slowly and can become worried if pushed too hard. Patience and consistency are required, as is a positive, confident attitude. Spoiling will create a pushy dog that lacks confidence, a combination that could be dangerous. Mature children are permissible provided *absolutely no roughhousing is permitted.*

This breed eats large quantities of food, an expense to consider. It may live ten to twelve years, but it is susceptible to bloat, hip dysplasia, eyelid abnormalities, gastrointestinal disorders, and respiratory problems. It snores and drools and is often flatulent.

Best Home: A large house in the country with a fenced yard or kennel is preferred, though this breed is easygoing in the home. The owner of a Bullmastiff must be a strong, easygoing, confident leader who is fully aware of the power of this breed and who does not project worry or concern. Macho types will create an unpredictable antisocial monster.

Time must be available to train, socialize, and handle this breed. Though very affectionate with its own pack, the Bullmastiff may be unpredictable and aggressive with your children's friends. Spoilers and weak, nervous, or overbearing people should avoid this breed, as should the elderly and the disabled.

Doberman Pinscher

Origins: A relatively new breed, the Doberman Pinscher was developed in the late nineteenth century in Germany. Created from Rottweiler, black and tan terrier, and perhaps German Shepherd and pointer bloodlines, it was bred to be a guardian, tracker, and companion and has served both the military and the police well.

Appearance: The Doberman Pinscher stands 24 to 28 inches at the shoulder and weighs between 60 and 100 pounds, though some breeders produce larger than normal Dobermans. It has a lean, muscular build, a docked tail, and cropped or uncropped ears. The shedding coat is short, glossy, and low-maintenance, requiring only occasional brushing. The color may be black, black with rust markings, reddish brown, or dark blue.

Breed Profile: This is an athletic, agile, playful, high-strung breed that, though dominant and territorial, can also be quite sensitive. Its macho attack-dog reputation is largely exaggerated; though very capable of doing protection work, this breed does not have the tough-guy demeanor of the Rottweiler.

The Doberman tends to be affectionate with its family and initially suspicious of strangers. It is a capable watchdog. Often an intense, excitable, stubborn breed, it needs a patient, consistent training style that is not overbearing. The Doberman can be passive-resistant, taking a head-in-the-sand attitude if pushed too hard, and it may snap if worried. Its excellent sense of smell acts as a distraction, making training a challenging task. Females tend to be more sensitive than the males and require a slower, less firm technique. Neutered males are often less aggressive and easier to train.

Obedience must begin early, be patient and precise, and include socialization and handling. The Doberman will not tolerate roughhousing from small children. We recommend this breed only for families with older, responsible children. The Doberman needs to be exercised daily to prevent restlessness and destructive behavior. Its lithe, strong physique and great endurance make it an excellent jogging partner. If left in a yard for long periods, a Doberman may dig and bark. It is also capable of jumping fences.

The Doberman Pinscher is susceptible to hip dysplasia, bloat, von Willebrand's disease (a blood disorder similar to hemophilia), and skin and heart problems. The Doberman can also be flatulent and can develop lick sores on its front feet if stressed. Because of its lean structure, pressure sores can develop on its body if it is not given a bed or blanket to sleep on. Avoid this breed if you live in a very cold environment, as it has little body fat and a very short coat.

Best Home: A house with a fenced yard or kennel is essential. The owner of a Doberman Pinscher must be an active, confident leader who prefers an athletic, high-energy dog. Overbearing, nervous, physically weak, and placating persons should avoid this breed, which, if spoiled, will lack confidence and possibly become a fear-biter. This highly sociable dog may become very stressed if left alone for extended periods. This is an excellent breed for a jogger to own. Older children are fine, but the elderly and the disabled might have dominance problems with this physically strong breed.

Giant Schnauzer

Origins: First used in Germany in the seventeenth and eighteenth centuries as a cattle and sheep drover, the Giant Schnauzer was created by crossing Standard Schnauzer, Great Dane, and Bouvier bloodlines. Its all-weather coat was developed to help protect it from cold, wet European weather. It has also been used as a guard dog and has worked with the military and the police.

Appearance: The Giant Schnauzer stands 23.5 to 27.5 inches at the shoulder and weighs between 65 and 95 pounds. It has a large, muscular body, a docked tail, and cropped or uncropped ears. The coat is wiry and harsh, the undercoat softer. Very little shedding occurs, but periodic clipping is necessary. If the dog is to be shown, however, it must be hand-stripped, a time-consuming procedure in which the dead hair is plucked out by hand to preserve the color and the hard, crisp texture of the coat. The color may be black or salt-and-pepper.

Breed Profile: The Giant Schnauzer is a serious, active, powerful breed that is affectionate and playful with its owners but initially reserved with strangers. Stubborn and rather single-minded, the Giant Schnauzer also has a moody, introspective side, similar to that of a Bouvier or a Scottish Terrier. It is a breed that needs to be constantly reminded of the rules of the house. It can become passive-resistant if pushed or required to do something it doesn't care to do. This attitude necessitates a firm yet precise, patient training technique that includes much positive reinforcement and early socialization. The females tend to be more passive-resistant than the males.

The Giant Schnauzer can be very protective, making it an excellent watchdog. Barking and digging will result if the dog is left in a yard all day. Regular exercise will keep this breed healthy and will help curb its restlessness.

The Giant Schnauzer tends to be dog-aggressive and has a high prey drive toward small animals. It will not tolerate roughhousing or hectic, unpredictable activity and is therefore not recommended for families with young children.

This breed can be susceptible to bloat and hip dysplasia.

Best Home: A house with a fenced yard is essential for this active breed. The owner of a Giant Schnauzer should be a strong, confident leader who is firm but patient and not overbearing. This dog is recommended for families only if the children are older, responsible, and capable of working the dog. Spoiling, nervous, and overbearing persons should avoid this breed, as should the elderly and the disabled. Time to train and socialize this breed must be available.

Great Dane

Origins: The Great Dane may have resulted from a cross between the ancient Mastiff and the Irish Wolfhound. It was first used as a hunting and guarding dog in northern Europe.

Appearance: The Great Dane is a huge, elegant breed, standing 30 to 34 inches at the shoulder and weighing between 120 and 165 pounds. The harlequin Danes, white with black patches, are the largest variation, whereas the brindle and fawn-colored Danes are more slender. The black Danes and the blues are usually somewhere in between. The body is massive, lanky, and well muscled, and the shedding coat is short, glossy, and of low maintenance, requiring only occasional brushing. The color may be black, black-and-white (harlequin), brindle, fawn, or blue-black. The ears can be cropped or uncropped.

Breed Profile: All Dane color variations have a similar temperament, the fawn and brindles perhaps being a bit more high-strung.

The Great Dane is truly enormous and is perhaps the most active of the giant breeds. Though not extremely intelligent, it tends to be a very affectionate family dog. The Dane can, however, be very suspicious of strangers. It is very territorial and often aggressive toward dogs or people. You may not want to choose a Dane if you have young children. The dog would love your children, but might be suspicious of their friends. Also, the Dane is capable of hurting a child during play, just by knocking them down, stepping on them, or hitting them with its tail.

Training should start early and should be firm but not overbearing. Be precise with a Dane, and take your time. Avoid confusing or worrying the dog. Remember also that all giant breeds mature slowly; a six-month-old will be huge but will still have the mind of a puppy.

We have found the fawn and brindle Danes to be slightly more sensitive and high-strung than the black and harlequins. Training technique should still be firm, but perhaps a bit slower and less demanding than that used with other breeds.

The Great Dane has a short coat and little body fat and therefore gets cold easily, so don't keep it outside too long during the winter. Provide it with a blanket or a bed to lie on so as to prevent pressure sores.

The Dane has an excellent sense of smell but below-average eyesight. Like the other giant breeds, it does not often live past eight or ten years of age. Many Danes have congenital heart problems as well as hip and shoulder problems. The Dane also has a habit of splitting open the tip of its big tail; it wags it with such enthusiasm that, when smacked against a door or cabinet, it will split open and bleed. This can be very messy. In addition, the Dane can develop lick sores on its front feet, particularly if it is kenneled for more than a week.

The Great Dane can suffer from bloat, a life-threatening gastric condition that can occur after a large meal. The stomach swells with gas and can actually twist upon itself, cutting off the blood supply to the digestive tract. Shock follows, and if not immediately treated by a vet, usually with surgery, the dog dies. At our facility, we avoid feeding Danes and other large breeds huge meals, splitting the daily feeding into two or three smaller meals. We also thoroughly soak the dry food in warm water for ten minutes so that no further expansion can occur in the stomach.

A Great Dane will eat eight to twelve cups of food a day, about three times what a small Lab would eat.

The Dane's size can be a problem with regard to transportation; it doesn't fit well into most cars, and if it needs to be transported by air, you will have to purchase the largest available airline crate, an expensive proposition.

Best Home: If you choose a Dane, make sure you have a large house with a big yard with a fence at least six feet high. The owner of a Dane should be a physically strong, confident, and easygoing leader. Physically weak, nervous, and spoiling types should avoid this breed, as should the elderly and the disabled. Dominant and territorial, the Dane can be very dog-aggressive, and needs strong leadership and socialization with people and other dogs from day one, if you want to avoid problems. This is important, for if a Dane becomes aggressive, no five people will be able to control it. Older, mature children who are physically capable of working the dog in obedience are okay. No roughhousing should be permitted at any time. Time to exercise this giant breed must be available on a daily basis.

Great Pyrenees

Origins: An old breed, the Great Pyrenees is believed to have originated in Cental Asia or Siberia. Migrating Germanic tribes brought this breed with them into Europe; herders in the Pyrenees Mountains between France and Spain came to rely on the Great Pyrenees as a master herd guarder that could protect sheep, goats, and cattle from wolves and bears. The all-weather coat and huge size made it perfectly adaptable to the job and the cold climate. The Great Pyrenees is still used today to guard herds in Europe and North America.

Appearance: The Great Pyrenees stands 25 to 32 inches at the shoulder and weighs 90 to 125 pounds. It is heavy-bodied and strongly muscled. The coat is long and thick with a soft, dense undercoat. It sheds, is highly absorbent of odors, and mats easily, requiring the owner to spend some time each day grooming. Some owners trim the coat to make grooming easier. The color is either pure white or white with gray or tan markings.

Breed Profile: This is an independent, reserved breed that is loyal and friendly only to its immediate family. It tends to be wary and suspicious of strangers, and has a strong guarding instinct typical to the breed. The Pyrenees has been bred to work, to protect, to defend. It is very territorial and not extremely sociable. Few breeds would be better at guarding your property and livestock than this one.

Dog aggression is a real problem with Great Pyrenees, however, and it is an instinctive, elemental ingredient in its makeup. For a thousand years this breed was asked to protect its herds from wolves; it is hard to change that innate distrust toward canines.

Training can be challenging. The Pyrenees tends to be stubborn and resistant and has been known to snap when irritated. A firm, no-nonsense technique is required. Again, consider the dog's instincts. It has been living with sheep herds, away from regular human interaction, for centuries. This has created a very independent mind-set that does not easily bend to the will of others. The "Come" command can be a difficult one to teach this breed.

In addition to early training, socialization with people in various different environments is important. Take the dog away from its home while it is still young and let it interact with people and dogs.

A Great Pyrenees may live for ten to twelve years. It can suffer from hip dysplasia, bloat, and eye infections. It may snore and drool, and it will eat large quantities of food.

Best Home: A sheep ranch in Montana is the best home for this breed. Barring that, a house in the country with a fenced yard is essential. The owner of a Great Pyrenees must be a strong, confident leader who desires a breed that will be reserved and territorial. Daily exercise is important. No nervous, spoiling, cautious, or overbearing persons should consider this breed. A job such as herding or tracking will give a Great Pyrenees purpose and will discourage restlessness and destructive behavior. Older children who are able to physically work the dog and gain its respect are okay, but roughhousing and hectic activity must not be tolerated. The elderly and the disabled should not consider this powerful breed, and those who live in warm climates should consider a breed with a less dense coat.

Komondor

Origins: An old herd-guarding breed from Hungary, the Komondor is known for its corded coat, which protects it from inclement weather and from the attacks of predators.

Appearance: The Komondor stands 23 to 27 inches at the shoulder and weighs between 80 and 120 pounds. It has a strong, thick, sturdy body. The dense, weather-resistant, shedding coat is long and is usually allowed to naturally combine with the undercoat to form moppish cords. These cords are highly absorbent of moisture and odor and can become mildewed if the dog spends time outside in wet weather. Cording is a high-maintenance style and is not very adaptable to the home; many choose instead to keep the coat clipped. The color is always white.

Breed Profile: This is a serious, purposeful herding breed that is not easily adaptable to family life. Wary, reserved, and very independent, the Komondor is normally affectionate only with its owners. This breed is very territorial and will not hesitate to show aggression toward a person or dog coming onto its property. A Komondor may also show aggression toward its owner if annoyed or pushed. This can be a downright nasty breed.

Training needs to start early and must be firm and uncompromising. A weak, placating owner will be easily overwhelmed by this dominant, independent breed, which, like the Great Pyrenees and the Kuvasz, was bred to live on its own with a herd of sheep with very little human contact. We do not recommend this breed for families with children or small animals.

Socialize a Komondor from day one and give it plenty of exercise to prevent destructive behavior.

The Komondor is susceptible to hip dysplasia and bloat.

Best Home: The best home for a Komondor is a sheep ranch in Montana. The second best would be a house in the country with a fenced yard. The owner should be a dominant, no-nonsense leader who wants an independent, protective breed and who has time to train, exercise, and socialize the dog. Weak, compromising, cautious owners will create a dominant, dangerous dog and may get hurt. This is not a dog for those with children, nor is it suitable for the elderly or the disabled.

Kuvasz

Origins: First seen in ancient Tibet and Turkey, the Kuvasz was perfected in medieval Hungary and used to guard herds, to hunt, and to protect its home. The original Kuvasz was considerably larger than to-day's dog.

Appearance: The Kuvasz stands 26 to 30 inches at the shoulder and weighs between 70 and 110 pounds. A powerful, big-bodied, lanky dog, this breed has a medium-length shedding coat and a soft under-coat. Regular brushing is required; the coat is highly absorbent of odors and will smell if the dog is kept outside. The only color is white.

Breed Profile: This smart, powerful athletic breed is similar to the Great Pyrenees and Komondor in function and in attitude. Dominant and very independent, the Kuvasz can be a difficult dog to own. It is very suspicious of strangers and is often dog-aggressive. Aggression when it comes is sudden; there is usually no posturing or warning beforehand. Because of the Kuvasz's stubbornness and strong guarding instincts, it is difficult to train this breed to adapt to a laid-back family lifestyle. Having friends or relatives over can be difficult, especially if the owners adopt a placating attitude toward the animal. The Kuvasz is also capable of being aggressive toward its own family.

Training must begin early and must be firm and consistent. The Kuvasz, though dominant and stubborn, can become worried and panicky if pushed too hard or fast, so take your time. Placating or spoiling this breed, though, could create an unconfident, pushy dog that is likely to bite.

The Kuvasz is susceptible to hip dysplasia and bloat. Its thick coat makes it a poor choice for those who live in warm climates. The breed also has the habit of splitting open the end of its tail by hitting it against walls or furniture. This can be hard to treat; the dogs may continue re-injuring the tail or chew-off the bandage.

Best Home: The best home for a Kuvasz is a sheep ranch in Montana. Barring that, a large house with a fenced yard is essential. The owner of a Kuvasz should be a physically strong, dominant, no-nonsense leader who desires a protective, reserved dog that may not be friendly toward strangers. We do not recommend this breed for families with children or pets, especially small ones. Weak, placating, or cautious owners should avoid this breed, as should the elderly and the disabled. Time to train, socialize, and handle this breed must be available. Daily exercise is essential for this breed to remain happy; without it, the dog may become restless and destructive. Those who live in warm climates should choose another breed.

Mastiff

Origins: The Mastiff, or Old English Mastiff, is one of the original ancient breed types, along with the hounds, herders, and Arctic types. Perhaps originating in Asia Minor (present-day Turkey), the Mastiff was distributed around the known world by Egyptian, Persian, Greek, and Roman armies and traders. Peasants in England kept this breed to ward off wolves and other predators. The Mastiff was bred for size, strength, protection, and courage.

Appearance: The Mastiff stands 27 to 32 inches at the shoulder and weighs between 150 and 200 pounds. Massive, large-boned, and muscular, the Mastiff is not quite as muscular as the Bullmastiff. Its shedding coat is short and coarse, with a dense short undercoat. Maintenance is low, requiring only periodic brushing. The color may be fawn, apricot, or brindle, usually with a black muzzle, ears, and nose.

Breed Profile: This laid-back breed has Herculean strength and a very protective attitude. The Mastiff is naturally dominant, courageous, and territorial and will be suspicious of strangers. Though affectionate with its owners and good with its own family's children, this breed may be suspicious of other children who come to visit. Even if the dog is playing happily, it can hurt a child because of its sheer size. The Mastiff can be quite aggressive toward other dogs and small pets.

Training should start early and should include plenty of socialization. Though this breed is stubborn and dominant, the training should be patient, precise, and never overbearing. A young Mastiff can become pouty and worried if pushed too hard. Remember that all giant breeds mature slowly; a six-month-old Mastiff may weigh 90 pounds but still have the mind-set of a puppy.

Though lethargic, the Mastiff does need daily exercise. It is not recommended, however, that you jog with this huge, heavy breed; the strain could eventually result in structural problems. It is also not advised to leave this breed alone in a yard all day; for this will accentuate its territorial instincts and encourage barking and digging.

It is essential to have uncompromising control over this powerful breed. When aggressive, a Mastiff can show explosive power with little warning. Strong confident leadership and plenty of socialization are mandatory.

The Mastiff is short-lived and is susceptible to hip dysplasia, bloat, heart problems, and eyelid problems. It eats large quantities of food and is therefore expensive to own. The Mastiff can also be flatulent.

Best Home: A large house with a fenced yard is essential. The owner of a Mastiff must be a strong, confident, patient leader who desires a dog with a protective nature. It is recommended for families only if the children are older and physically able to work the dog in obedience. Placating, cautious, and physically weak persons will create a pushy dog that lacks confidence and may have the propensity to bite. Harsh, overbearing types should also avoid this breed, as they might create a fearful mind-set that could result in aggression. The elderly and the disabled should avoid this powerful breed. Time to train, socialize, and exercise this breed must be available.

Newfoundland

Origins: Possibly the result of a cross between the Great Pyrenees and the Labrador Retriever, this giant breed was used by fishermen in Newfoundland to help haul in nets, to rescue drowning victims, to pull carts, and to perform retrieval tasks in the water. Its large body and insulative coat keep it warm and allow it to swim in icy water.

Appearance: The Newfoundland stands 26 to 28 inches at the shoulder and weighs between 100 and 150 pounds. It has a large, powerful body, webbed feet, and a medium-length flat, glossy shedding coat with a soft undercoat. Daily brushing is essential to prevent matting. The color may be black, chestnut, or black-and-white (Landseer). The Landseers in our experience tend to be slightly smaller than the black or chestnut Newfoundlands.

Breed Profile: This strong, powerful, water-loving breed has a sweet, playful disposition. Though initially suspicious of strangers, it quickly warms up to most people and is not nearly as territorial as the Mastiff or Great Pyrenees. It will function adequately as a watchdog and may show some aggression toward strange dogs.

The Newfoundland is more trainable than the Mastiff, perhaps due to the influence of retriever bloodlines. Training technique should be firm and consistent, but not overbearing, and should start early, as should socialization. Remember also that giant breeds mature slowly; a six-month-old Newfoundland may weigh 80 pounds but will still have a puppy mind-set.

The Newfoundland is very active for a giant breed and must be exercised daily. Swimming should be incorporated into the dog's life, as should retrieving. The only drawback to a daily swim is the potential mess it can make of your home afterward; make sure you have the time and patience to dry and brush this breed after a swim. Depending on the cleanliness of the water, the dog may need to be bathed as well.

The Newfoundland makes a good family pet and usually loves children. Care must be taken, however, that this giant does not knock small children down during play. Roughhousing should be discouraged.

The Newfoundland is short-lived and is susceptible to congenital heart disorders, bloat, hip dysplasia, and eyelid problems. It drools, snores, and eats very large amounts of food, making it an expensive pet to own.

Best Home: A house with a fenced yard is essential. The owner of a Newfoundland should be an active, patient, confident leader. Weak, placating, nervous, and overbearing persons should avoid this breed. Children are fine, provided no roughhousing is permitted. Time for training, exercise, grooming, and socialization must be made available on a daily basis. A nearby swimming area would be a plus. The Newfoundland does well in cold weather, but may have trouble in the heat. The elderly and the disabled may have trouble controlling this large, gregarious breed.

Portuguese Water Dog

Origins: Used for centuries by Portuguese fishermen to retrieve lost gear and to herd fish into the nets, this old breed, with its webbed feet and waterproof coat, has a great affinity for the water. The Poodle, Irish Water Spaniel, and Portuguese Water Dog all sprang from the same genetic beginnings.

Appearance: The Portuguese Water Dog stands 17 to 23 inches at the shoulder and weighs between 35 and 60 pounds. It has a muscular, athletic body and is slightly smaller than the Irish Water Spaniel. Two coat types exist, curly and wavy. The curly version consists of tight Poodle-like curls; the wavy coat is straighter with more luster. Both types shed very little and need to be brushed two or three times a week. The wavy coat is sometimes clipped from mid-back to rump, with the hair at the end of the tail left long. The curly coat is often kept about an inch long over the entire body. Either type can be cut in this style. The color may be black, white, brown, or brown-and-white.

Breed Profile: An active dog, the Portuguese Water Dog tends to be reserved with strangers, preferring its own family. It loves the water and should have access to it on a regular basis. Sometimes a worrier, this breed needs consistent, patient, precise training and socialization from early on. Overbearing techniques may cause this sensitive breed to bite. Though similar to the Irish Water Spaniel in temperament, it tends to be slightly less playful and clownish. It will not tolerate hectic, unpredictable activity and is not the best choice for families with young children.

The Portuguese Water dog is susceptible to hip dysplasia and to a rare neurological disorder known as storage disease, a fatal condition that is characterized by Parkinson-like tremors.

Best Home: A house with a fenced yard is essential. This active dog needs an active, confident leader with time available to train, exercise, and socialize. Nervous or placating persons will reduce this sensitive breed's confidence level, thereby encouraging fear aggression. Families with young children should avoid this breed. The elderly and the disabled may have trouble dealing with this breed's activity level. Access to a swimming area is a plus.

Rottweiler

Origins: An ancient mastiff-type breed, the Rottweiler was used by Roman legions to herd and guard flocks of sheep taken along on campaigns as a food supply for the soldiers. It was later used as a cattle drover and guard dog in Germany.

Appearance: Rottweilers stand 22 to 27 inches at the shoulder and weigh between 70 and 120 pounds. Size varies according to sex. Powerful and thickly muscled, the Rottweiler has a big-boned body and a coarse mid-length coat that sheds but is relatively easy to maintain, requiring brushing once or twice a week. The tail is docked.

Breed Profile: Certain breeds such as the Cocker Spaniel, Dalmatian, and Chinese Shar-Pei sometimes reach a cultish level of popularity. When this occurs, demand creates a plethora of unethical breeders who care only about earning a fast buck, and who produce dogs of questionable physiology and temperament. Over the last decade, this has happened to the Rottweiler.

The Rottweiler is a large, heavily muscled dog possessing strength, courage, and average intelligence. It is by nature one of the most territorial breeds. Highly suspicious of strangers, the Rottweiler will guard its owner's house and yard with savagery if necessary. It should not be kept in a place where people often walk by, such as a chain-link fence next to a sidewalk. This will encourage it to fence-fight and become aggressive. Keep this breed inside your house, where it can guard your home more effectively.

Do not tie a Rottweiler up. This is the easiest way to bring out aggression and frustration.

The Rottweiler is extremely dominant and pushy, and likes to use its big body to control you by leaning and pushing on you. Don't mistake this for affection; it is control. This breed requires a strong, no-nonsense leader and firm, early training. Socialization also needs to begin early on. We never recommend these dogs to families with children. We often see Rottweilers showing aggression toward their own families when leadership is severely lacking. A child who gets scared and runs screaming from a Rottweiler will stimulate the dog's natural instinct to run down its prey.

The Rottweiler doesn't like to be handled, particularly on its feet. You must start doing this early on, and you must clip its nails at least twice a week, starting when it is a puppy. If you don't, you will create an avenue for its innate dominance to sneak in.

A confident, well-bred Rottweiler that has received firm early training and has not been spoiled can be a satisfactory pet, but unfortunately many of the ones we see now are insecure, flighty, physical abominations. Bad breeding by avaricious types, combined with the actions of ignorant buyers whose reasons for choosing this breed are frequently suspect, have helped to create this problem. There is nothing more dangerous than a 110-pound insecure, fear-biting male Rottweiler.

Let us clarify one thing: when acquired from a diligent breeder and trained properly, a Rottweiler can be an admirable, courageous, loyal dog capable of a high level of obedience. And yes, there are good, caring breeders out there who have suffered because of the careless breeding going on. Our sympathies go out to them. But as it stands, the despicable quality of the American Rottweiler today forces us to refuse recommending it, especially to families with children.

The Rottweiler often suffers from hip dysplasia and shoulder problems. It is therefore important to investigate the health of the parents, particularly the status of their hips. Structural problems can be exaggerated by allowing the dog to become overweight, so do not let this happen. Hip or shoulder pain in a Rottweiler may not be discernible to an owner because this breed can tolerate pain quite effectively, but this pain-masking can result in aggression toward the owner when the dog does not want to be touched in a sensitive area.

The Rottweiler puppy is very susceptible to canine parvovirus, a highly contagious viral disease that attacks bone marrow, intestinal, lymph, and heart cells. A puppy infected with parvo usually dies; the only way to prevent it is through vaccination. We recommend an additional parvo booster shot at twenty-two weeks of age for the Rottweiler in addition to the normal schedule of shots.

Best Home: A house with a fenced yard or kennel is essential. Do not leave a Rottweiler in the yard all day, however. The owner of a Rottweiler must be a strong, firm, uncompromising leader who sets rules and sticks to them. Do not consider this breed if you are nurturing, placating, disabled, or elderly, if you have children, or if you don't have enough time to work the dog. An untrained Rottweiler left in the yard all day is an accident waiting to happen. Also, do not get more than one at a time, and do not get littermates. They will bond more closely to each other than to you and create behavioral nightmares.

If you live by yourself and want a dog you can feel safe with, a Rottweiler might be for you. No one will bother you if you are walking a big male Rottweiler at night. Don't jog with one; it is too heavy and may develop structural problems.

You must prove your leadership every day to a Rottweiler. This is not macho posturing on our part; it is the truth. If you disregard this advice, you or someone else could get hurt.

If you choose a Rottweiler, spend lots of time finding a good breeder. Visit several before you decide. See the parents, and really take your time. Consider a female; they tend to be less aggressive. Socialize and train! And if you have children, get a Golden Retriever.

Saint Bernard

Origins: Saint Bernard established a refuge for weary travelers in the Swiss Alps around the eleventh century. In the seventeenth century, monks living at the refuge recruited some Saint Bernard dogs as companions and guard dogs; they soon discovered that the dogs were quite adept at finding lost travelers, due in part to

their excellent sense of smell and their great size, which allowed them to efficiently clear pathways through the snow. Once they located their victim, the dogs' enormous size provided warmth enough to sustain the victim until help arrived.

Before its use as a rescue dog in the Alps, the Saint Bernard was used by the Romans and was probably first brought to Switzerland by them (Roman armies were responsible for the wide distribution of many breeds).

Appearance: The Saint Bernard stands 25 to 30 inches at the shoulder and weighs upwards of 180 pounds. It is an enormous, powerful, and big-boned breed. There are two versions, the longhaired and the shorthaired. There are no discernible behavioral differences between the two, the longhaired coat requiring only slightly more grooming. Both shed. The color may be red-and-white, brown-and-white, or brindle-and-white.

Breed Profile: The Saint Bernard has a good nose, which, as in the scent hounds, can pose a challenge with regard to maintaining focus in the dog. This and its tendency to be a bit stubborn and slow are the major obstacles to training. A firm yet patient training technique is required. Remember that giant breeds mature slowly; a six-month-old Saint Bernard may weigh 100 pounds, but it will have a puppy mind-set, so go slow.

Don't underestimate this dog's size and strength. A disobedient Saint Bernard will drag you down the street six blocks, stop to relieve itself, then drag you another eight blocks. This can be embarrassing, not to mention dangerous.

A well-bred Saint Bernard is a mellow, affectionate, lazy dog; it will protect your home, but not with the same ferocity as a Bullmastiff or a Rottweiler. A fairly quiet breed, it normally gets along well with other people and dogs. Of the giant breeds, the Saint Bernard and the Newfoundland are possibly the friendliest and best with children. The Saint Bernard can make a good family dog, but it must be obedience-trained early because of its tremendous size. Like any giant dog, it can hurt a child without meaning to. We do recommend that you have ample room for this breed, although we have known of people in New York City apartments who have owned them.

There are drawbacks. Like other giant breeds, the Saint doesn't live long. Eight to ten years is all you should expect. This breed is also prone to heart problems, bloat, and, because of its size, hip and shoulder problems. Don't let it get fat, and don't run with it. Hip surgery on this breed is very expensive. This breed also snores and drools, the males more than the females (there is an ongoing attempt to breed a "dry mouth" Saint Bernard).

Best Home: A large house with a fenced yard is preferable. The owner of a Saint Bernard should be a firm, patient, confident leader who prefers a lazy, friendly, slow-thinking behemoth of a pet. A weak, placating, or nervous owner may create a pushy dog that lacks confidence. Overbearing people could create a worried pet capable of fear-based aggression. Children are fine, provided no roughhousing occurs.

The elderly, the disabled, and the diminutive may have trouble controlling this breed. Also, keep in mind that this breed will eat eight to twelve cups of food a day—an expensive proposition if the dog is eating quality food.

Samoyed

Origins: An ancient Siberian breed, the Samoyed was used by the nomadic peoples of the same name, to guard herds of reindeer and to pull sleds. This hardy breed has remained relatively pure for centuries.

Appearance: The Samoyed stands 19 to 23.5 inches at the shoulder and weighs between 45 and 65 pounds. It has a strong medium-size body that is graceful and athletic and a face that seems always to be smiling. The undercoat is thick, soft, and insulating; the harder, straight outer coat grows through the undercoat. Shedding is year-round, particularly in early summer. Daily brushing is required. If this breed is left outside, its coat may become matted and odorous. The color is white or off-white.

Breed Profile: This is an intelligent, alert, highly independent breed that, though friendly, can be a challenge to train. It has a sassy, impetuous side to its personality that is endearing yet troublesome. It is by nature a dominant, controlling breed that may become pushy and unruly if not given proper leadership.

Training, which can be difficult due to the Samoyed's independent, stubborn nature, must begin early and must be firm and consistent. The Samoyed will resist surrendering control and is capable of showing aggression toward its owners, particularly if they have been too lenient. Establishing dominance is the key to owning a Samoyed. Any spoiling will increase the chances of dominance aggression. We have seen many Samoyeds take over as alpha leader of their pack, using bites, barking, and tantrums to get their way. We do not recommend this breed for families with young children. The most difficult command to teach, as with all northern breeds, is the Come. In addition, handling must occur every day so as to facilitate conflict-free grooming. If you wait too long, this breed will learn to be intolerant of brushing and may bite in protest.

The Samoyed can be a good watchdog. It barks more than most breeds—often to the point of irritation. We have seen a number that have been de-barked, a procedure we do not approve of. If left in the yard all day, it may bark, dig, and become a matted mess.

Make sure this breed gets enough daily exercise. Without it, the dog may become restless, destructive, and loud.

The Samoyed is susceptible to hip dysplasia and does not do well in warm climates.

Best Home: A house with a fenced yard is essential, though this breed should not be left in a yard all day. The owner of a Samoyed must be an active, strong, dominant leader and must enjoy a breed that, though intelligent, will be a challenge. Time to train, socialize, and groom the dog must be available daily. Passive, placating persons will have control problems with this breed, perhaps resulting in a dominant, pushy animal capable of biting friends or family.

We don't recommend this breed for those with small children. Older children must not be allowed to roughhouse or to play chase games with this dog, and they should be capable of working with the dog in obedience. The elderly and the disabled may have trouble establishing dominance over this breed and should consider one only if they are physically capable of training, exercising, and grooming it every day.

Siberian Husky

Origins: Bred in Siberia for use as sled dogs, this smart medium-sized breed has great stamina and a lively, independent nature. Its thick, insulating coat protects it against the bitter cold.

Appearance: The Siberian Husky stands 20 to 23 inches at the shoulder and weighs between 35 and 60 pounds. The females tend to be much smaller than the males. It has a medium-sized athletic body and a high-maintenance coat that sheds copiously and requires regular brushing. The undercoat is dense, giving the dog great insulation against the cold. In the spring the Husky loses much of this undercoat. Don't get a Husky if you are allergic to dog hair! Eye color for the Huskie is variable. Blue is common, as is brown. Often one of each is seen.

Breed Profile: Mushers actually have minimal contact with their sled dogs, especially during inclement weather, unlike those who work with retrievers, which rely and thrive on regular close contact with humans. A breeds that performs its task with less human control tends to be more intelligent and on the stubborn, independent side. This definitely describes the Husky.

"Independent" is a politically correct way of saying that a breed very likely to tell you to stuff it if it feels it's got something better to do. The Husky loves to roam and run and do its thing. It can be very resistant to training, particularly with regard to the Come command. The same slightly belligerent attitude also makes them rather personable. This is not the same type of stubbornness you might find in an Airedale, which will become passive-resistant and just stick its head in the sand when resisting your commands. The

Husky can be a real character, and when it so chooses, it is loving and sweet, making it a good family dog.

The Siberian Husky has some other unique traits. It is very clean and rarely gives off any doggy odors. It is also very vocal, not barking so much as yodeling in howls and yips similar to the vocalizations of wolves. This can be annoying and hard to modify.

Smart but obstinate, the Husky is not the easiest breed to train. It needs lots of exercise and would not be a good choice for an apartment dweller. It is also a poor watchdog, quite likely to take off at the first sign of trouble. Because of its love of running, this breed can make a great jogging partner, provided the weather is not too warm.

The Husky is normally friendly to almost anyone and is usually good with children. Being able to get out and run once a day is also important to a Husky. When you do this, make sure there are no cats, small dogs, or squirrels around, because the Husky has a very high prey drive and can be rather aggressive toward small dogs and other small animals. If you are walking your Husky and a squirrel or a Toy Poodle runs by, hold on to the leash for dear life.

The Husky can be prone to hip dysplasia and chronic diarrhea. It seems to have a gastrointestinal tract that can overreact to changes in diet or environment. Put a Husky on one type of food and don't change it unless you're advised to do so by your vet. Also, avoid kenneling a Husky for long periods of time; it may not eat well, may get diarrhea, and may suffer from what we call kennel fever, a restless state of mind that is best described as a claustrophobic dread of confinement. Try instead to get someone to house-sit for you.

Best Home: A house with a fenced yard is essential. The owner of a Siberian Husky should be a firm, competent leader who likes a playful, challenging, independent breed. If you like personable, affectionate, obstinate dogs that shed a lot and like to run and eat squirrels, then this is the dog for you. Spoilers, nervous types, and overbearing persons should avoid this breed. Time to exercise and train—especially the Come Command—is essential. Children are okay, but no roughhousing should be allowed. Small animals could pose a problem due to this breed's high prey drive. The elderly and the disabled may have trouble with this active, impetuous breed.

Standard Schnauzer

Origins: Of the three Schnauzer variations, this is the oldest, dating back to fifteenth- and sixteenth-century Germany. It is thought that Poodle, spitz, and pinscher bloodlines were crossed to develop this breed. The Standard Schnauzer has been used as a ratter and a guard, as a police and military dog, and as a companion.

Appearance: The Standard Schnauzer stands 17 to 20 inches at the shoulder and weighs 30 to 45 pounds. Sturdy and compact, it has a medium-sized body, a docked tail, and cropped or uncropped ears. The coat is of medium length, wiry, thick, and weather-resistant, and it sheds very little. Coat color is either silver/gray or black. Periodic brushing and clipping are necessary. Show dogs must be hand-stripped, a lengthy process in which dead hair is pulled out by hand rather than clipped so as to preserve the hardness and luster of the coat.

Breed Profile: The Standard Schnauzer is fiesty, intelligent, and driven. Though affectionate with its owners, it is not always eager to please and can be suspicious of strangers, making it a good watchdog.

Though training can be difficult, the Standard is easier to train than the Miniature or the Giant Schnauzer. Most terriers have an agenda all their own, which usually does not include listening to their owners at crucial moments. A firm, consistent technique must be used, but training must not become rushed or overbearing. The Come and the Down-Stay are often difficult commands to teach. Though not as moody as the Giant Schnauzer, the Standard will become passive-resistant, taking a head-in-the-sand attitude, if pushed too fast or too hard. In addition to the training, this breed should be socialized and handled from puppyhood.

The Standard Schnauzer can be noisy and, if not exercised daily, may become restless and destructive. If left in a yard, it may dig large holes. It also has a high prey drive and may therefore be aggressive toward small dogs and other small animals.

This is a long-lived breed. The Standard Schnauzer can be susceptible to hip dysplasia.

Best Home: The Standard Schnauzer can live in an apartment if exercised daily, but it may bark at strange noises, which could get you evicted. If you have a fenced yard, don't leave the dog in it for long periods; it will dig and bark. The owner of a Standard Schnauzer should be an active, firm, confident leader who is patient and precise with training and who desires an active, independent, plucky dog. Time to socialize, exercise, and handle the dog on a daily basis must be available. Passive or placating persons could create a dominant, cantankerous dog that might bite family or friends. Overbearing types should avoid this breed; tough treatment could create a fear-biting pet. Older children are okay provided no roughhousing occurs. The elderly and the disabled can own this breed provided they are able to train, socialize, and handle it properly.

The Terrier Group

Breeds in the Terrier Group are sturdy, courageous, driven dogs originally bred to hunt rodents and other burrowing mammals. They are very independent and have a high prey drive. Though capable of great obstinacy, terriers can make good house pets.

Airedale

Origins: Derived from crossing old English black and tan terrier with Otterhound bloodlines, the Airedale was first used in nineteenth-century England for big game hunting, vermin killing, and police and military work.

Appearance: The Airedale is the tallest of the terriers, standing 22 to 23 inches at the shoulder and weighing between 50 and 60 pounds. It has a strong, muscular, sturdy body and a wiry, low-maintenance, non-shedding coat that requires periodic clipping. Show dogs, however, need hand-stripping, a process that involves pulling dead hair out by hand to preserve the luster and hard texture of the coat. Color is normally black-and-tan, with some red and, less often, white markings.

Breed Profile: This strong, athletic breed exhibits all the tenacity and determination of a terrier, only in a larger-than-usual package. The Airedale is stubborn and is often difficult to train. It learns slowly, so don't expect one to pick up on things as quickly as a German Shepherd or a Border Collie.

The Airedale is active, sometimes flighty, and often sensitive to the demands of training. If an Airedale resists learning a certain command, the last thing you should do is get firmer with the dog. Its resistance will only increase and could accelerate into panic. It should not be babied, either; a crystal-clear, incremental training technique needs to be implemented from an early age.

Though affectionate with its owners, the Airedale tends to be suspicious of strangers and can show aggression toward people and dogs. Because it is territorial, it makes a good watchdog. The Airedale cannot always discriminate between friend and foe, however, and it may give your friends and your children's friends a hard time. We do not recommend this breed for families with young children, and we strongly recommend early obedience training and lots of socialization with people and other dogs from an early age.

Best Home: A house with a fenced yard is essential. The owner of an Airedale should be a strong, confident leader who combines firm discipline with patience and precision. Persons considering this breed should desire a dog that has an active, tenacious temperament and is reserved with strangers. Nervous or placating persons will create a pushy, obnoxious dog that lacks confidence. Overbearing types may bring out fear-aggressive behavior.

The Airedale needs daily exercise and makes a good jogging partner because of its athletic physique. If left alone for long periods, it might become destructive and noisy.

This breed has a high prey drive, so watch it around small animals.

The Airedale may not tolerate the hectic, unpredictable behavior of young children. Older children are okay, provided they can gain the animal's respect by working it in obedience. The elderly and the disabled may have trouble controlling this active, driven breed.

American Staffordshire and Staffordshire Bull Terrier

Origins: Both the American Staffordshire Terrier and the Staffordshire Bull Terrier were originally bred as fighting dogs. They have unparalleled jaw strength, biting mechanics, and courage. Produced by crossing the fierce nineteenth-century Bulldog with various terriers, the Staffordshires were used in England and in this

country as pit fighters, taking on other dogs in vicious contests that normally ended in death for one or both contestants. Most responsible breeders are currently aiming for a more docile temperament.

Appearance: The American Staffordshire Terrier stands 17 to 19 inches at the shoulder and weigh between 55 and 70 pounds. The smaller Staffordshire Bull Terrier stands 14 to 16 inches at the shoulder and weighs between 30 and 40 pounds. One is almost a smaller carbon copy of the other. Both are densely muscled, particu-

larly in the neck and shoulder area. They have tremendously strong jaw muscles that bulge out like chewing tobacco in a baseball player's cheeks. Ears are cropped or uncropped. Their short, stiff, shedding coats are low maintenance and often feel prickly to the touch. The color may be fawn, black, fawn-and-white, black-and-white, or brindle.

Breed Profile: These dogs should not be confused with the type of animal known as the "Pit Bull Terrier." The Pit Bull Terrier is recognized by the United Kennel Club but not by the American Kennel Club and will be discussed later in this book. Here we are discussing only the American Staffordshire Terrier and the Staffordshire Bull Terrier, breeds that are similar to each other in temperament, differing mainly in size. The American Staffordshire Terrier (AST), as we said above, is a larger, heavier dog than the Staffordshire Bull Terrier (SBT).

Both breeds have largely been given a bum rap. A combination of media sensationalism, careless breeding, and irresponsible owners have combined to create a troublesome situation. Make no mistake: in the wrong hands, these two breeds could be perverted into machines of destruction. However, when obtained from an ethical breeder, and properly trained and socialized, they are affectionate, sensitive pets.

These breeds are active dogs, owing to their terrier-Bulldog ancestry. They are intelligent and affectionate and, though dominant and rather pushy, tend to be more sensitive than other dominant breeds such as the Bullmastiff. Training them is a challenge because of this pushy yet sensitive character.

Both the AST and the SBT have a high prey drive, great determination, and extreme tenacity. These qualities, when improperly handled, can be dangerous. The dogs' prey drive can cause an improperly socialized, poorly bred animal to kill other animals or to attack a child that is running and screaming. Unfortunately, there are cowards out there who create sociopathic dogs in order to bolster their own failing egos; they get one of these breeds, name it Cujo or Hitler, and teach it to attack, to intimidate, to hate. These persons are the ones who have helped generate the infamous reputation. They breed substandard dogs on a whim in their yard or basement, and sell the flawed animals to other insecure, posturing idiots who continue the cycle. They have created public fear and hatred of a breed that has many redeeming qualities.

If you are considering an AST or SBT, first examine your motive. If it is to intimidate or to be perceived as cool, then put this book down and get a life. If you are mature and responsible, then first find some top-notch breeders, not some heroin dealer living in a condemned building. Good breeders are out there; you just have to look hard and be willing to spend a good amount of money for a quality dog. The breeder should not be reluctant to let you see the parents of the pups as well as the rest of the litter. He or she should also be willing to put you in touch with previous customers.

Socialization is of paramount importance with these dogs. Get the puppy out among people and other animals as soon as possible and do so on a regular basis. Obedience training is an absolute must, starting early and continuing through adulthood. Unless these dogs have good genetics, socialization, and training, we simply cannot recommend them to families. They may love you and your children, but they will be unpredictable around all others.

Never tie an AST or SBT up, and never keep them in a yard where people are walking by constantly, as this can bring out aggression that you may not have seen otherwise. Never keep them in a place where children can tease them.

Even a well-bred AST or SBT can become dog-aggressive; remember their heritage, and structure their lives accordingly. Also, when these dogs bite, it's for keeps. So do not encourage this type of behavior!

Do not own more than one AST or SBT at a time. Two or more of these dogs often adopt a non-thinking mind-set that, when combined with their high prey drive, can result in trouble, particularly with regard to aggression toward other dogs. Once these dogs go into aggressive mode, they are nearly impossible to stop.

Amstaffs and Staffordshire Bulls are susceptible to hip dysplasia.

Best Home: A house with a fenced yard or kennel is essential. These dogs are strong, affectionate, high-energy animals that demand potent, patient leadership, free of posturing, egoism, or machismo. Overbearing, macho persons should avoid these breeds, as should nervous, weak, or placating types, the elderly, and the disabled. An owner of either breed should prefer an affectionate, very active dog that needs structured activity and frequent exercise. Because these breeds have a high prey drive, there should be no small animals in the household. Time to train and socialize must be available.

Australian Terrier

Origins: First used in nine-teenth-century Australia as a ratter, snake killer, and watch-dog, the Australian Terrier is a mixture of various rough-coated terriers, including the Skye, Cairn, Norfolk, and York-shire.

Appearance: The Australian Terrier stands 10 to 11 inches at the shoulder and weighs between 10 and 18 pounds. It has a compact, sturdy body and is short-legged in proportion to its body length. The tail is docked. The coat is hard and straight, with a softer undercoat. Shedding is minimal, as is the level of mainte-nance. The color may be blue-and-tan, sandy, or reddish brown.

Breed Profile: The Australian Terrier is smart, alert, and busy and possesses keen senses. Normally reserved with strangers, it is very affectionate with its owners and makes an excellent watchdog. Like other terriers, this breed can be stubborn and will be challenging to train. Its attention is easily diverted by distractions, particularly a small animal or a person wandering into its territory. Hardy in personality, the Australian Terrier responds well to early, firm, pre-cise training techniques. It will accept older children, but may not be tolerant of the unpredictability of young children. Roughhous-ing could elicit a warning bite and should not be allowed. Possibly dog-aggressive, this breed also has a high prey drive toward small animals such as cats and rabbits. The Australian Terrier is long-lived and has no serious health problems.

Best Home: An apartment is fine, provided this breed is walked several times a day. The owner of an Australian Terrier should be a confident, capable leader who enjoys an active, intelligent, and sometimes impetuous dog. The Australian Terrier does well with the elderly and the disabled, provided it is obedience-trained early and not spoiled. A spoiled terrier often becomes a biter, because, like most dogs, it interprets spoiling as a recognition of its dominance. A dog that has been made the center of attention may become dominant and may use biting as a disciplinary technique, not realizing that it is an undesirable behavior.

Older children are fine with this breed, provided there is no roughhousing. Time to train and socialize must be made available. If left alone too long, an Australian Terrier may bark and dig incessantly.

Bedlington Terrier

Origins: Used in the early nineteenth century in England as a hunter of badgers, foxes, and rats, the Bedlington Terrier was also unfortunately used for dog fighting because of its high prey drive and dog-aggressive tendencies. Today it is a companion.

Appearance: The Bedlington Terrier stands 15 to 17.5 inches at the shoulder and weighs between 17 and 25 pounds. The body is thin, athletic, and muscular with a slightly arched back and long legs. The coat sheds little and is composed of hard and soft curls. Brushing is required once or twice a week, and clipping every eight to ten weeks. The Bedlington is normally cut in a distinctive lamblike fashion, with the hair on its head cut in a domed style. Colors include bluish white, tan, and brown.

Breed Profile: Though easygoing around the house, this breed is known to be one of the most dog-aggressive of the terriers. Its high prey drive and historic dislike of other dogs seems to have stayed with it through the years. The Bedlington is tenacious and not entirely trustworthy around other animals.

The Bedlington Terrier has the stubborn attitude toward training that is typical of most terriers. It is prey-driven, not pack-driven like a retriever. Dominant by nature, the Bedlington wants to interact with people on an equal basis. The challenge with this or any other terrier is to get it to respect you as the authority figure. Training must be firm and consistent but not overbearing and must include socialization with people and dogs from puppyhood on. The Come command is difficult to teach this breed. Spoiling a Bedlington may result in a dog that thinks biting is a valid option, so do not do it.

The Bedlington may not be tolerant of small children and may bark and dig incessantly if left alone in a yard.

Best Home: An apartment is adequate, provided the dog is exercised daily. The owner of a Bedlington Terrier must be a strong, confident leader who desires an active breed that is reserved with strangers. Time to train and socialize must be made available. Spoilers and those with meek personalities could create a dominant, suspicious, nasty animal. Only children old enough to work the dog in obedience are acceptable. The elderly and the disabled can own this breed if they are able to train and exercise it.

Border Terrier

Origins: One of the oldest terriers, the Border Terrier was used in Great Britain to hunt fox and badger. It is a spunky, athletic dog bred to have endless stamina and determination.

Appearance: The Border Terrier stands 9 to 11 inches at the shoulder and weighs between 11 and 15 pounds. The body is compact and sturdy. Its legs are long, enabling it to keep up with dogs of much larger size. The short, weather-resistant coat is coarse and wiry, sheds little, and requires very little care. Show dogs should be hand-stripped, a lengthy plucking procedure that preserves the texture and luster of the coat. The color may be wheaten, blue-and-tan, or reddish brown, with black-tipped hairs dispersed throughout.

Breed Profile: This is a very active breed with tenacity and great drive. Perhaps the most personable of the terriers, the Border seems to have a greater desire to please than other breeds in this group. This affectionate breed generally shows aggression only if spoiled. The Border Terrier can be dog-aggressive if not socialized properly, however, and will have a high prey drive toward small animals. Training should be consistent, patient, and never overbearing, as this breed does have a sensitive side to it.

Like any other terrier, this breed can be a challenge. If you have the patience, though, the Border Terrier will make a great companion.

Best Home: If properly trained, the Border Terrier can make a good apartment dog, provided it gets plenty of exercise. The owner of a Border Terrier should be an active, competent leader who prefers a high-energy, playful dog. The Border Terrier loves children and will play tirelessly with them, but young children should be instructed not to roughhouse. The elderly and the disabled can own this breed provided they are able to train and exercise it. Spoilers and meek types may cause this breed to become pushy and nippy. This breed loves to dig, so do not leave it alone in a yard for long periods of time. Overbearing types may cause this breed to worry and exhibit fear-aggression. Time to train and socialize must be made available.

Bull Terrier and Miniature Bull Terrier

Origins: The Bull Terrier and Miniature Bull Terrier first appeared in England in the late nineteenth century. They are said to be a cross between the old Bulldog, the now extinct English Terrier, and the Spanish Pointer. Though initially used as a fighting dog, the Bull Terrier is now a companion. The Miniature Bull Terrier is a scaled-down version of the Bull Terrier and is similar in temperament.

Appearance: The Bull Terrier stands 15 to 22 inches at the shoulder and weighs between 40 and 75 pounds. The Miniature stands 10 to 14 inches at the shoulder and weighs 10 to 20 pounds. Both have thickly muscled, squat, bullish physiques, sunken eyes, and domed foreheads. The shedding coat is short, harsh, and almost prickly to the touch and requires a brushing once a week. Colors are white or "colored," which means any color other than white, brindle being the most popular.

Breed Profile: The Bull Terrier and the Miniature Bull Terrier are active dogs that are affectionate and playful with their owners but reserved with strangers—Spuds MacKenzie is not typical of the breeds. Often stubborn, the Bull Terriers can sometimes show an unpredictable aggressive side that belies their smiling faces. Dogs of both sizes can be quite dog-aggressive, and they have a high prey drive toward small animals such as cats and rabbits. The aggression problem is more serious with the Bull Terrier due to its larger size and strength.

Training should begin early with these breeds and it should be firm and precise but not overbearing. If pushed too hard, these dogs may get snappy. Go slow; the Bull Terriers do not learn quickly and can become passive-resistant, taking a head-in-the-sand attitude. Socialization is also recommended from an early age.

We do not recommend the Bull Terrier as a family dog. The Miniature should be fine with families provided no roughhousing is permitted.

Both breeds are susceptible to hearing problems, eyelid abnormalities, and skin disorders.

Best Home: Both the Bull Terrier and the Miniature can live in an apartment, but the larger Bull might be happier in a house with a fenced yard. Either breed should be owned by a firm, competent leader. These are active, potentially aggressive dogs that cannot be owned by meek or spoiling types. We do not recommend the Bull Terrier for families with children. The Miniature can live in a family with older children, but no roughhousing should occur. The elderly and the disabled should avoid the Bull Terrier but could own the Miniature provided they are able to exercise and train the dog.

Cairn Terrier

Origins: Developed in Scotland, the Cairn Terrier was used as a ratter and as a bolter of foxes and otters. The weather-resistant coat allowed this breed to withstand the cold, windy Scottish climate.

Appearance: The Cairn Terrier stands 9 to 10 inches at the shoulder and weighs between 12 and 15 pounds. A strong, solid little dog, the Cairn has a rough, weather-resistant coat that sheds little and requires minimal brushing and clipping. Any color but white is acceptable; the most common are wheaten, dark gray, and dark brindle, all with black-tipped hairs dispersed throughout the coat.

Breed Profile: The Cairn is in many ways the archetypal terrier, exhibiting the same tenacious, sassy, obstinate yet endearing personality so common to this group. Smart, active, and affectionate, the Cairn is sometimes reluctant to cooperate with its trainer, but it is certainly more willing and trainable than a Miniature Schnauzer or an Airedale. This breed is a barker, but not to the same degree as a Schnauzer or a Wire Fox Terrier.

The Cairn is initially suspicious of strangers and makes a good watchdog. It has a high prey drive toward small animals; bringing a kitten or hamster home might not be a good idea. With training the Cairn can be a good family pet, but it will not tolerate children the way a Pug or a Dachshund might. No roughhousing should be allowed. The Cairn can be a nipper, particularly when spoiled or in one of its pouty, resistant moods, which often come when learning the Down command, a hard command for any terrier to learn. The Cairn can make an excellent companion for an elderly or disabled owner.

The Cairn Terrier is a long-lived dog and is not susceptible to any major medical problems.

One more thing: if you choose a Cairn, please don't name it Toto.

Best Home: An apartment is fine if the dog is walked several times a day. Be aware, though, that this breed can be a barker. The owner of a Cairn should be a fair, competent leader who desires an active, feisty, impetuous little dog that will be initially suspicious of strangers. Spoiling may create a nasty, pushy dog that bites. Time to train, exercise, and socialize should be available. The Cairn is good with older children, provided no roughhousing is permitted. The elderly and the disabled can own this breed provided they can train and exercise it.

Dandie Dinmont Terrier

Origins: This breed was named after a character in Sir Walter Scott's nineteenth-century novel *Guy Mannering*. Scott's Dandie Dinmont was a farmer who owned six of these feisty dogs. This breed's low-slung stature suggests that there may be Corgi or Dachshund in its lineage. Dandies were originally used as ratters.

Appearance: The Dandie Dinmont Terrier stands 8 to 11 inches at the shoulder and weighs between 18 and 25 pounds. It has a low, sturdy, strong body and a short, wavy, hard and soft coat that sheds little and requires only periodic brushing. A clipping every two to three months is needed. Show dogs need to be hand-stripped, a plucking procedure that preserves the texture and luster of the coat. The color is either pepper (blue-black) or mustard (reddish brown to light fawn).

Breed Profile: This feisty terrier is intelligent and strong-willed and seems to believe it is a much larger dog. Though affectionate with its owner, the Dandie will be suspicious of strangers and other dogs. As a result, it makes an excellent watchdog. It has a high prey drive, which would make owning a rabbit or cat difficult. Training needs to be firm and consistent; any spoiling will make this breed dominant and perhaps nasty.

A Dandie Dinmont may not tolerate young children. Older children must not roughhouse and should participate in the training in order to gain the dog's respect.

If left in a yard for too long, this breed may bark and dig.

Because the Dandie Dinmont has a long back and short legs, it can develop back and leg problems, including arthritis and osteitis if overworked or overweight.

Best Home: An apartment is adequate for a Dandie if the dog is walked regularly. The owner of a Dandie Dinmont should be a firm, consistent leader who will not spoil or placate the dog. Nervous or overbearing types may incite aggression and should avoid this breed. Time for training and socialization must be available daily. Older children are acceptable, provided they participate in the training and do not roughhouse. The elderly and the disabled can own a Dandie if they are able to train and socialize it.

Fox Terrier, Smooth

Origins: Used in England in the eighteenth century as a bolter of fox and as a ratter, this breed is now considered a separate breed from the Wire Fox Terrier. Greyhound, Beagle, Wire Fox, and Bull Terrier may have been used in the development of the Smooth Fox.

Appearance: The Smooth Fox Terrier stands 14 to 15.5 inches at the shoulder and weighs between 15 and 20 pounds. It has a strong, athletic body and a smooth, short, shedding coat that requires only periodic brushing. The color is white with black or brown patches.

Breed Profile: The Smooth Fox Terrier is an amusing, lively, and very independent breed. Like all terriers, it tends to be feisty and at times defiant. The Smooth Fox Terrier has a higher than normal prey drive for a terrier and may be very aggressive toward other dogs and suspicious of strangers. It is often hard to focus this breed's attention, especially when other animals are present.

Training must start early and be firm and consistent. Down and Come are the most difficult commands to master with this stubborn, willful breed. Socialization is also important; get the dog out among people and dogs when it is a puppy. Spoiling may create a dominant, pushy animal that uses biting to get its way.

The Smooth Fox, unlike the other terriers, loves to retrieve. Use this as a method of focusing the dog's attention and as a constructive exercise. Smooth Fox Terriers may not be tolerant of small children, and no one should be allowed to roughhouse with these dogs.

Best Home: An apartment is adequate if the dog is given daily exercise, but a house with a fenced yard is better for this highly active terrier. The owner of a Smooth Fox Terrier should be a confident, capable, patient leader who prefers a very active, feisty breed over a couch potato. Spoilers and nervous types should avoid this breed, as these attitudes can often create a dominant, aggressive mind-set in the dog. Older children are fine provided they take part in the training. The elderly and the disabled can own this breed if they are able to train, socialize, and exercise it. There should be no small animals in the home.

This breed needs constructive exercise every day. Retrieving, jogging, or agility work will give its busy mind something to focus on. Without activity the dog may become restlessness and destructive.

Fox Terrier, Wire

Origins: Used in eighteenth-century England as a bolter of foxes and as a ratter, the Wire Fox Terrier is now considered a separate breed from the Smooth Fox Terrier. The rough-coated black and tan terrier and the Smooth Fox are both in this breed's ancestry.

Appearance: The Wire Fox Terrier stands 14 to 15.5 inches at the shoulder and weighs between 15 and 20 pounds. It has a strong, athletic body and a short, wiry coat with a soft undercoat. Some shedding occurs. Periodic brushing and clipping are required. Hand-stripping, a plucking procedure that preserves the texture and luster of the coat, is required for show dogs. The color is white with black or tan patches.

Breed Profile: The Wire Fox Terrier, though almost identical to the Smooth in behavior, does exhibit some interesting differences. Like the Smooth, it is lively, feisty, and very independent, but its obstinacy is more detached. The Wire Fox often seems to enter a world all its own, where it is sometimes hard to reach. The Wire Fox also tends to be a slightly slower learner than the Smooth, perhaps because of its more distractable nature.

The Wire Fox Terrier has a very high prey drive and is more dog-aggressive than the Smooth; it is perhaps the most combative terrier aside from the Bedlington. It will be suspicious of strangers and makes a good watchdog. It barks and digs, often incessantly, and should not be left in a yard for long periods.

Training must start early and be firm and consistent. The Down and Come are the most difficult commands to teach this stubborn, willful breed. Socialization is paramount; get the dog out among people and dogs when it is a puppy. Spoiling may create a nasty, pushy animal that uses biting to get its way.

Wire Fox Terriers like to retrieve, so use this as a method of focusing the dog's attention and as a constructive exercise. A Wire Fox Terrier may not be tolerant of small children, and no one should roughhouse with it.

Best Home: An apartment is adequate if the dog is given daily exercise, but a house with a fenced yard is better for this active terrier. Do not leave it in the yard for long periods, though; it may bark incessantly or dig its way out. The owner of a Wire Fox Terrier should be a confident, capable leader who prefers an active, feisty breed over a couch potato. Spoilers and nervous types may create a dominant, nasty mind-set in the dog. Older children are fine provided they take part in training the dog. The elderly and the disabled might have trouble with this active breed.

This breed needs constructive exercise every day, be it retrieving, jogging, or agility work. Without activity the dog may become restless, destructive, and noisy.

Irish Terrier

Origins: This old Irish breed was used as a ratter and hunter of small game that could also work as a retriever on land or in water. The Irish Terrier was also used as a messenger dog during wartime.

Appearance: The Irish Terrier stands 17 to 18 inches at the shoulder and weighs between 25 and 30 pounds. It has a strong, leggy body and a short, dense, wiry coat that sheds little and requires only periodic brushing and an occasional clipping. Show dogs must be hand-stripped, a time-consuming hair-plucking technique that preserves the texture and luster of the coat. The coat may be any one of several shades of red.

Breed Profile: Though a curious, spirited, active breed, the young Irish Terrier tends to be sensitive, like the Airedale. Puppy training must therefore not be overbearing or rushed. Because the Irish is more thoughtful and personable than the Wire Fox Terrier, a patient, consistent training technique combined with early socialization is advised. An adult Irish Terrier will be more confident and perhaps a bit stubborn, requiring a slightly firmer training attitude.

The Irish Terrier can be suspicious of strangers and may show some aggression toward other dogs. It makes a good watchdog and should be okay with older children if they participate in the training.

The Irish Terrier needs daily exercise to stay healthy and well behaved. If restless, it may bark and dig incessantly. This is a good breed to jog with given its trim, athletic physique.

Best Home: An apartment is adequate if the dog is exercised daily, but a house with a fenced yard is better. Do not leave it in the yard for too long, however, or it may bark and dig. The owner of an Irish Terrier needs to be a confident leader capable of dealing with an active breed that is both obstinate and sensitive. Overbearing persons may panic a young Irish Terrier and may incite an older dog into fear-based aggression. Spoiling this breed will encourage uncontrollable, pushy behavior. Older children capable of participating in the training are okay. The elderly and the disabled can own this breed provided they are able to train, exercise, and socialize it.

Kerry Blue Terrier

Origins: First used in Ireland in the eighteenth and nineteenth centuries as a ratter, a hunter of small game, a retriever, and a herder, the Kerry Blue Terrier was considered an all-around utility dog. Though now mainly a companion dog, it is still a capable ratter.

Appearance: The Kerry Blue Terrier stands 17 to 20 inches at the shoulder and weighs between 35 and 40 pounds. It has a strong, sturdy body and a short, curly coat that sheds little but requires periodic brushing and needs to be clipped every two to three months. The blue-black or gray coat usually lightens somewhat with age.

Breed Profile: This active, athletic terrier tends to be suspicious of strangers and usually shows affection only toward its immediate family. The Kerry Blue is stubborn and requires a firm, consistent training technique. The Stay and Come commands are the most difficult to teach.

The Kerry Blue sometimes exhibits the same moody, passive-resistant attitude seen in the Bouvier des Flandres and the Giant Schnauzer. Early socialization is essential, as is daily exercise. This is an excellent breed to jog with if it has been well trained and has learned to respect its owner's leadership. If not, it may show aggression toward other dogs or joggers along the way. Dog-aggression can be common with all terriers because of their high prey drive and territorial nature.

This breed may not tolerate the unpredictable behavior of small children.

The Kerry Blue may be restless and noisy if left alone for too long. It may also dig.

Best Home: A house with a yard is preferable but not essential if the dog is exercised enough. The owner of a Kerry Blue Terrier should be a firm, confident leader with patience and persistence and should appreciate an active, athletic, and often stubborn breed. Spoiling, meek, or nervous types may create a pushy dog capable of biting to get its way. Overbearing persons could incite fear-aggressive behavior. Older children who can participate in the training process should be okay. Time must be made available to train, socialize, and exercise the Kerry Blue. The elderly and the disabled can own this breed only if they are capable of training and exercising it. It may be difficult to keep small pets such as cats or rabbits in a home with a Kerry.

Lakeland Terrier

Origins: The Lakeland is an old working terrier from the Cumberland County region of England, an area studded with beautiful lakes. It was bred to hunt fox and otter and is related to the Bedlington Terrier.

Appearance: The Lakeland Terrier stands 14 to 15 inches at the shoulder and weighs between 15 and 20 pounds. It has a strong, sturdy body and was bred with a narrow rib cage to enable it to squeeze into the rocky dens of otters. The tail is partially docked. The coat is weather-resistant, wiry, and coarse with a softer undercoat. It sheds little and requires only periodic brushing and a clip every few months. Show dogs should be hand-stripped to preserve the texture and luster of the coat. The colors may be black-and-tan, blue, black, liver, or wheaten.

Breed Profile: The Lakeland Terrier is an active, agile breed that is not as high-strung as the Wire Fox Terrier. Though affectionate with its owners, it can be suspicious of strangers and may show aggression toward other dogs. It has a high prey drive toward small animals.

The Lakeland is similar to the Airedale and the Irish Terrier in that it is sensitive to overbearing training techniques, particularly when it is young. Though stubborn, it must nevertheless be trained using a slow and precise method. The Come and Stay commands are the most difficult to teach.

The Lakeland Terrier may not tolerate the unpredictable behavior of young children.

Do not leave this breed alone for too long, especially in the yard. It may become restless and may dig and become very noisy.

Best Home: An apartment is adequate if daily exercise is provided. The owner of a Lakeland Terrier must be confident, patient, and precise and must desire an active, busy dog. Time to train, socialize, and exercise the dog must be made available. Spoilers may end up with an obnoxious, snappy animal. Overbearing types may incite fear-based aggression. Older children are fine provided they do not roughhouse and are able to participate in the training process. The elderly and the disabled can own this breed if they are able to train and exercise it.

Manchester Terrier, Standard

Origins: Developed in eighteenth- and nineteenth-century England by crossing Whippet, terrier, and possibly Dachshund bloodlines, the Manchester Terrier was used for ratting and for rabbit coursing.

Appearance: The Standard Manchester Terrier stands 15 to 17 inches at the shoulder and weighs between 12 and 22 pounds. It has a strong, sleek, athletic body, cropped or uncropped ears, and a short, smooth, easy-care shedding coat. The color is always black-and-tan.

Breed Profile: The Manchester is an intelligent, personable, high-strung, busy breed that tends to worry about strangers and unpredictable situations. Though bossy, it is not as controlling as the Miniature Pinscher. Strangers should not be encouraged to pet this breed until it has accepted their presence. The Manchester may not tolerate the unpredictability of young children. In addition, this breed may be dog-aggressive and will have a high prey drive toward small animals.

Training should begin early with this stubborn breed, and the trainer must be be firm and consistent but not overbearing. Spoiling this breed will create a pushy, nippy, obnoxious attitude.

The Standard Manchester Terrier is a good watchdog, but it can be noisy and may dig if left unattended in the yard.

Best Home: An apartment is adequate if the dog is walked several times daily. The owner of a Manchester Terrier should be a firm, consistent leader who prefers a busy, intelligent, slightly impertinent dog. Spoiling will create an obnoxious, potentially nasty dog. Though not tolerant of small children, this dog will accept older children who do not roughhouse and who participate in the training. Watch the Manchester around small pets such as cats or rabbits. The elderly and the disabled can own this dog if they are able to train and exercise it properly.

Miniature Schnauzer

Origins: Schnauzers are a very old German breed, dating back to the fifteenth-century. The Miniature Schnauzer came about by crossing small Standard Schnauzers with Affenpinscher and Poodle bloodlines. Initially used as a ratter, it is now considered a companion dog.

Appearance: The Miniature Schnauzer stands 12 to 14 inches at the shoulder and weighs between 13 and 18 pounds. It has a sturdy, compact body that is proportionately identical to that of the Standard. The tail is docked, and the ears may be cropped or uncropped. The wiry outer coat is harsh, and the undercoat is soft. Some shedding occurs. This breed requires regular brushing and needs to be clipped every few months. Show dogs need to be hand-stripped to preserve the texture and luster of the coat.

Breed Profile: The Miniature Schnauzer is a feisty, playful, active breed that is currently the most popular of the terriers. Though not as reserved as the Standard or Giant Schnauzer, the Miniature tends to be spoiled more often and therefore can be somewhat more impetuous and pushy. Its inquisitive, precocious nature is endearing, but can make training difficult. Firm, consistent training and early socialization are necessary. The Miniature Schnauzer may not tolerate small children.

Miniature Schnauzers make good watchdogs, but they may be dog-aggressive, and they have a high prey drive toward small animals. If left alone in a yard for too long, they may bark and dig.

This breed can live fifteen to twenty years, but may develop skin allergies and tumors later in life.

The Miniature Schnauzer is a popular breed, so be very selective when picking a breeder. *Do not buy from a pet shop.*

Best Home: An apartment is adequate if the dog is walked several times daily. Remember, though, that this breed can be noisy. The owner of a Miniature Schnauzer should be a firm, consistent leader who desires an active, personable, curious dog. Any spoiling will encourage bossy, snappy, aggressive behavior. Time to train and exercise the dog should be available. Older children who can help train and who do not roughhouse are fine. The elderly and the disabled can own this breed, provided they are able to train and exercise it.

Norfolk Terrier and Norwich Terrier

Origins: Developed in nineteenth-century England for use as ratters, these two spirited terriers share a common ancestry and differ only in the carriage of their ears.

Appearance: The Norfolk Terrier and the Norwich Terrier stand 9 to 10 inches at the shoulder and weigh between 10 and 12 pounds. They have small, sturdy bodies, docked tails, and short, wiry, weather-resistant coats that shed little and require only periodic brushing and an occasional trim. The color may be reddish brown, wheaten, or black-and-tan. The ears are dropped in the Norfolk and pricked in the Norwich.

Breed Profile: Active, feisty, and curious, these two breeds embody the true terrier nature. Affectionate with their owners, they tend to be initially reserved with strangers, and can be dog-aggressive. They both have a high prey drive toward small animals and should be watched around cats, birds, and pet rodents. They make great watchdogs and can bark with the best of them.

Though intelligent, these terriers can be stubborn and will initially resist training. The challenge will be overcoming their tendency to be easily distracted. A firm, consistent training technique should be used from puppyhood on; any spoiling could incite obnoxious, snippy behavior. Socialize them from puppyhood on, and get them used to being handled. Neither breed will easily tolerate the unpredictability of young children.

Though some say that the Norwich is slightly more outgoing than the Norfolk, we have not seen any discernible difference between the two.

Best Home: An apartment is fine if the dog is walked several times a day. The owner of a Norfolk or Norwich Terrier should be an active, competent leader who enjoys a feisty, busy, curious dog. Spoilers will create a bossy, snippy, dominant animal. Neither breed will tolerate excessive handling from young children. Older children are fine, provided they do not roughhouse and do help train the dog. Time to train, socialize, walk, and handle these dogs must be available. The elderly and the disabled can own either of these breeds if they are able to train and exercise them.

Scottish Terrier

Origins: Clearly identifiable as a breed in the eighteenth-century, the Scottish Terrier was first used in the Scottish Highlands as a ratter and a hunter of fox.

Appearance: The Scottish Terrier stands 9 to 10 inches at the shoulder and weighs between 18 and 22 pounds. It has a strong, compact, thick-boned body with short legs, prick ears, and a short, wiry coat with a softer undercoat. It sheds very little and requires only a quick daily brushing and a clip every three months. Show dogs are hand-stripped to preserve the texture and luster of the coat. The color may be black, dark gray, brindle, or wheaten.

Breed Profile: The Scottie is less busy and more serious than most other terriers. Though affectionate and personable with its own family, it is very discerning about other people and can be downright sullen at times. A one-or two-person dog, it is likely to be dog-aggressive and suspicious of strangers. Many Scotties act like irritable, grouchy old men or women.

Training should start early and must be firm and consistent but not rushed or overbearing. A Scottie can become passive-resistant, taking a head-in-the-sand attitude if pushed too fast or hard, and may bite if it feels it is being treated unfairly. Never spoil a Scottie; it may become bossy and snippy. Socialization, starting in puppyhood, is essential if you want the dog to be comfortable around your friends. We do not recommend this breed for families with small children.

A Scottie makes a good watchdog. It may bark and dig if bored or left alone for too long.

Do not overfeed a Scottie. It can put on weight easily, which may cause its long, low frame to suffer structural problems.

Watch out for skin allergies with this breed.

Best Home: An apartment is fine if the dog is walked several times daily. The owner of a Scottish Terrier should be a firm, consistent leader who is patient and not overbearing and who desires a breed that is very particular about the company it keeps. A quiet, predictable environment is preferable. Spoiling a Scottie will create a bossy, potentially aggressive dog. Older children who do not roughhouse and who help with training should be okay. The elderly and the disabled can own this breed if they can train and exercise it.

Sealyham Terrier

Origins: Developed in Wales in the nineteenth-century, this terrier was used to hunt badger, otter, fox, and other vermin.

Appearance: The Sealyham Terrier stands 10 to 11 inches at the shoulder and weighs between 20 and 24 pounds. Its sturdy, strong, short-legged body is similar to that of the Scottish Terrier. The ears are folded and the tail is docked. The medium-length coat sheds little, is wiry and coarse, and has a softer undercoat. Regular brushing is necessary, as is a clip every three months. Show dogs are painstakingly, hand-stripped to preserve the texture and luster of the coat. Color is white, often with lemon or tan markings on the ears and head.

Breed Profile: This active, independent but not extremely busy terrier is similar to the Scottish Terrier in temperament, though without the same degree of moodiness. It is reserved with strangers and can be dog-aggressive. It has a high prey drive and will chase small animals.

Because the Sealyham tends to be stubborn, it needs training and socialization early on. Technique should be firm and consistent but not overbearing. Any spoiling will encourage bossy, nippy behavior. This breed may not tolerate the unpredictability of small children.

The Sealy tends to be a barker and a digger, especially if left in a yard all day.

Do not overexercise or overfeed a Sealyham. Its low, long physique can be overloaded, and the dog may ultimately develop arthritis or spinal problems.

Best Home: An apartment is adequate provided the dog is walked several times a day. The owner of a Sealy should be a confident, capable leader who desires a bold dog that is somewhat less active than other terriers.

Spoilers will create a bossy, nippy dog. Overbearing types will encourage fear aggression. Older children are okay, provided they help in the training and do not roughhouse. The elderly and the disabled can own this breed, provided they are able to train and exercise it.

Do not leave a Sealyham alone in a yard for too long, and monitor it around any small pets such as cats or rabbits.

Skye Terrier

Origins: Developed in seventeenth-century Scotland on the rocky Isle of Skye, this vermin-killer was bred low to the ground to afford it access to the tight dens and burrows of rodents. Its long coat served as protection against the bites of its prey.

Vital Statistics: The Skye Terrier stands 9 to 10 inches at the shoulder and weighs between 20 and 25 pounds. It has a long, low-riding, powerful body, "teddy bear" ears, and a long, straight, medium-to high-maintenance shedding coat with a soft undercoat. It has a sheepdog-like beard and a curtain of hair covering its face and eyes. Brushing and combing is necessary every day. The coat is very absorbent and will smell and mat easily if not kept dry. A shorter pet clip would make maintenance easier. Colors include black, blue, gray, and cream.

Breed Profile: Though active and independent, this breed is not as busy as other terriers. The Skye Terrier will be affectionate with its owners, but it can also be moody and stubborn and is usually reserved with strangers. Not a dog to be pampered, this breed needs firm, consistent training early on, as well as extensive socialization and handling. The Skye can become passive-resistant, taking a head-in-the-sand attitude, and it will be especially difficult on the Stay and Come commands. If pushed too hard, the Skye may bite.

Like most terriers, the Skye has a propensity to dig and bark, can be dog aggressive, and has a high prey drive toward small animals. It makes a good watchdog and needs only two or three walks a day to remain happy and fit. Over-exercising a Skye can result in back and leg problems.

The Skye Terrier will not tolerate the unpredictability of young children.

Best Home: An apartment is fine, provided the dog is walked several times a day. The owner of a Skye Terrier should be a firm, consistent leader who desires a somewhat discriminating, introspective terrier. A quiet, predictable home is best. Spoilers may create a nasty, controlling animal. Overbearing types may encourage fear-based aggression. Older children who are able to help with training are okay. No roughhousing should be tolerated. The elderly and the disabled can own this breed if they are able to train and walk it. Time to train, socialize, groom, and walk this breed must be available.

Soft-Coated Wheaten Terrier

Origins: Developed in the early eighteenth century in Ireland, this medium-size breed was used for ratting, hunting badger and rabbit, and herding.

Appearance: The Soft-Coated Wheaten Terrier stands 17 to 19 inches at the shoulder and weighs between 30 and 40 pounds. It has a strong, agile, medium-size body, a docked tail, and a medium-length wavy coat that is finer and softer than the coats of other terriers. The shedding, absorbent coat can mat and become malodorous if allowed to remain wet. Daily brushing is necessary, as is a trim every few months. The color is always wheaten.

Breed Profile: Gentler and sweeter than other terriers, the Soft-Coated Wheaten, though friendly, can be initially reserved and timid around strangers. The training technique used with this active but considerate breed needs to be less demanding and more patient than those used on other terriers.

The Soft-Coated Wheaten needs a great deal of positive reinforcement and confidence building from puppyhood on. Socialization in different venues is necessary to overcome this breed's tendency to worry over new situations. Demanding and overbearing training techniques could bring about fear-based aggression, so take your time with this breed, and be as confident as you can in its presence.

The Wheaten is normally good with considerate children. If you do have children, consider acquiring a male dog, which will be less timid and more outgoing. This breed may bite out of worry or panic and may be dog aggressive. It also has a high prey drive toward small animals.

Select a Soft-Coated Wheaten carefully. Make sure its parents are outgoing and friendly. Don't pick a puppy that shows any fear or timidity.

Best Home: An apartment is adequate if the dog is exercised daily. The owner of a Soft-Coated Wheaten should be a calm, patient leader, with no overbearing tendencies. Spoilers and nervous types will reduce the confidence level of this breed and encourage fear-based aggression. Respectful children are okay, provided no rough-housing occurs. The elderly and the disabled can own this breed provided they are able to train and exercise it. Time to train and socialize this sensitive breed must be available. Watch the dog carefully if you have small animals in your home, because the Wheaten does have the prey drive of a terrier.

Welsh Terrier

Origins: This very old breed was developed in Wales to hunt otter, fox, and badger. The Welsh Terrier's direct ancestor, the black and tan terrier, was the progenitor of many terrier breeds.

Appearance: The Welsh Terrier stands 14 to 15.5 inches at the shoulder and weighs between 18 and 22 pounds. It has a sturdy, athletic medium-size body, a docked tail, and a short, wiry, low-maintenance coat that sheds little, requires minimal brushing, and needs to be clipped every three months. Show dogs require hand-stripping, a plucking procedure that preserves the texture and luster of the coat. The color is black with reddish tan.

Breed Profile: Bold and spirited, the Welsh Terrier is similar to the Airedale in appearance, and in its sensitivity to overbearing or rushed training techniques when young. It is reserved around strangers, can be dog-aggressive, and has a high prey drive. The young Welsh may be timid and in need of lots of confidence-building and positive reinforcement.

Though sensitive, this breed is also stubborn and requires precise, persistent guidance. It processes information slowly and may get confused if pushed too fast.

The Welsh Terrier may not appreciate the unpredictability of young children.

This breed needs regular exercise to remain happy. If left in a yard for too long, it may dig and bark incessantly.

Best Home: An apartment is adequate if the dog is exercised regularly. The owner of a Welsh Terrier should be a firm, patient leader who prefers an active, curious, sensitive breed. Spoilers and nervous types could create a pushy dog that lacks confidence and may bite. Older children who can help with the training and don't roughhouse are okay. The elderly and the disabled can own this breed provided they are able to train and exercise it. Time to train, exercise, and socialize the dog must be available.

West Highland White Terrier

Origins: Developed in Scotland during the eighteenth and nineteenth centuries, this ratter has the same roots as the Cairn Terrier.

Appearance: The West Highland White Terrier stands 10 to 11 inches at the shoulder and weighs between 15 and 20 pounds. It has a small, sturdy body and a medium-length straight coat that is not as harsh as the Cairn's. It sheds little, requires brushing twice a week, and should be clipped every three months. Show dogs require hand-stripping, a plucking procedure that preserves the texture and luster of the coat. If not brushed and kept dry, the coat will mat. The color is always white.

Breed Profile: Though sassy, the Westie is not quite as feisty as the Cairn. It is stubborn, independent, very personable, and affectionate to its owner. Suspicious of strangers, it makes a good watchdog. Though intelligent, it can be challenging to train due to its independent nature. The Westie is more thoughtful and trainable than a Fox, Irish, or Welsh Terrier, but it needs firm, consistent training, socialization, and handling from early on.

This breed tends to be a barker and may dig incessantly if left in a yard. It has a high prey drive toward small animals. A Westie may not tolerate the antics of young children and may bite if handled roughly. The West Highland White Terrier may suffer from skin allergies, but it is long-lived.

Best Home: An apartment is fine if the dog is walked several times a day. The owner of a West Highland White should be a firm, consistent leader who enjoys an active, personable, and sometimes impetuous breed. Spoilers and nervous or meek types may encourage a bossy, nippy attitude in the animal. Overbearing types might encourage fear-biting. Older children who can help with the training are okay. No roughhousing should be tolerated. The elderly and the disabled can own this breed if they are able to train and exercise it.

Section Six

The Toy Group

Dogs in this group, such as the Maltese and the Toy Poodle, were bred to be companion dogs and lapdogs. They are small in comparison to other breeds. Some are only 4 inches tall at the shoulder and weigh just 2 or 3 pounds. Though delicate, they tend to be long-lived, and are very often spoiled half to death. Most toys are difficult to housebreak, and most are picky eaters.

Affenpinscher

Origins: Developed in seventeenth-century Germany, this terrierlike toy was once kept as a ratter in stores and on farms.

Appearance: The Affenpinscher stands 9 to 11.5 inches at the shoulder and weighs between 6 and 8 pounds. It has a compact, sturdy body, a docked or undocked tail, cropped or uncropped ears, and a short, harsh, low-maintenance coat that sheds little and needs to be brushed two or three times a week. The long hair surrounding the face gives it a monkeyish look. The color may be black, gray, clack-and-tan, or reddish tan.

156

Breed Profile: The Affenpinscher is an active, intelligent, excitable toy dog with lots of terrierlike nervous energy. It is an inquisitive breed that is affectionate with its owners and suspicious of strangers. It is often dog-aggressive.

The Affenpinscher is stubborn, and will resist training, which must start early and be firm, consistent, and not overbearing. Early socialization will help reduce this breed's suspicious nature and improve its confidence. Spoiling will create a nervous, snappy animal. Like other toys, this breed may be hard to housebreak. It tends to bark quite a lot and will dig if left in a yard.

The Affenpinscher is susceptible to extremes of temperature and may develop respiratory problems. It wheezes and may snore.

Best Home: An apartment is fine provided the dog is walked several times a day. Bear in mind, however, that it may bark a lot and may get you evicted. The owner of an Affenpinscher should be a firm, patient leader who desires a feisty, active, terrierlike toy dog. Spoilers may create a pushy, nasty dog that lacks confidence. Overbearing types may encourage fear-aggression. Older children who participate in the training are okay, provide that no roughhousing occurs. The elderly and the disabled can own this breed if they can train and walk it. Other small pets in the home are not recommended, though a cat should be able to take care of itself. Time to train, housebreak, and socialize the Affenpinscher must be available.

Brussels Griffon

Origins: Developed in Belgium in the eighteenth and nineteenth centuries this companion dog is a mixture of Affenpinscher, Pug, and spaniel bloodlines.

Appearance: The Brussels Griffon stands 9 to 10 inches at the shoulder and weighs between 9 and 12 pounds. It has a sturdy terrierlike body, a docked tail, and a face like that of a little werewolf. The coat can be rough or smooth. The rough coat is wiry, hard, and short; the smooth coat is short, glossy, and straight. Both types shed little and require only periodic brushing and a clip every three or four months. Show dogs must be hand-stripped, a plucking procedure that preserves the texture and luster of the coat. The colors may be black, black-and-tan, red, and beige.

Breed Profile: This breed, like the Affenpinscher, has a terrierlike demeanor, though it is perhaps not as stubborn or high-strung. Affectionate with its owner, a Brussels Griffon may be initially reserved with strangers and will be a good watchdog. It may be dog-aggressive, and it has a high prey drive toward smaller animals.

Training should start early and must be consistent and precise. Though stubborn, this breed can be sensitive to rushed or overbearing training techniques. Spoiling may create a pushy, nippy attitude and will lower the dog's confidence level. Socialization is important and should begin in puppyhood. Older children who participate in the training process are okay, provided no roughhousing occurs.

The Brussels Griffon has a tendency to bark and dig and can be difficult to housebreak. It is also susceptible to extremes in temperature. Wheezing and snoring are common.

Best Home: An apartment is fine provided the dog is walked regularly. The owner of a Brussels Griffon should be a patient, precise leader who enjoys a busy, amusing, terrierlike toy dog. Spoilers may create a pushy, nippy dog that lacks confidence. Older children who help train are okay. The elderly and the disabled can own this breed if they can train and walk it. Time to train, housebreak, and socialize must be available.

Chihuahua

Origins: A very old breed dating back to the time of the Aztecs, the Chihuahua, originating in South and Central America, has been a companion to kings and commoners for centuries.

Appearance: The Chihuahua stands 6 to 9 inches at the shoulder and weighs 6 pounds or less. This is a truly small, delicate breed. It may be smooth-coated or long-coated. Both coats shed little and require only periodic brushing. The coat may be any color and may be solid or patched.

Breed Profile: The long-coated and smooth-coated Chihuahuas have similar temperaments. They are fairly nervous, high-strung dogs that are affectionate with their owners but tend to worry over strangers and other dogs. They are not comfortable in new environments and tend to be happier when left at home. The Chihuahua dislikes unpredictable, hectic activity and will not tolerate young children or roughhousing. It is a good watchdog that can be quite boisterous and yappy when provoked, but this trait can make it a difficult dog to have in an apartment, however.

The Chihuahua can be very hard to housebreak. It will resist obedience training and may become nippy when threatened or annoyed. Training should begin early and be firm but patient. Socialization is important as a confidence-building technique. To be fair, much of the undesirable behavior seen in this breed—and in most of the toys—is as a result of spoiling by owners who forget that Chihuahuas are dogs and not squirrel monkeys.

The Chihuahua needs minimal exercise and can be a loving companion for someone who leads a quiet life.

If you choose a Chihuahua, bear in mind that it may live a long time, like the other toys. It will get underfoot and can be hurt if stepped on. The Chihuahua is very sensitive to extremes in temperature and may need a sweater on a cold day.

Best Home: An apartment is fine, though this breed can be very noisy. A few trips outside each day will provide ample exercise. The owner of a Chihuahua should be patient, confident leader who desires a spunky, busy toy that has discriminating taste in people. Spoiling this breed may create a bossy, nippy, noisy pain in the neck. The Chihuahua is not tolerant of children. The elderly and the disabled make very good owners provided they are able to train. Time to properly housebreak, train, and socialize must be available.

Chinese Crested

Origins: Though the age of this breed is not clear, it is thought to have been developed by the Chinese in the seventeenth-century from the bloodlines of African hairless dogs. It has always been a companion dog.

Appearance: The Chinese Crested stands 11 to 13 inches at the shoulder and weighs between 6 and 10 pounds. Its body is fine-boned and delicate. It comes in two versions, hairless and powderpuff. The hairless variety has no coat aside from the silky tufts on its head, tail, and feet. Unlike all other breeds, the hairless has sweat glands on its body. The powderpuff variety has a medium-length silky, soft, shedding coat that requires only periodic brushing. Colors include white, brown, black, tan, and various color combinations.

Breed Profile: The Chinese Crested is an intelligent, alert, inquisitive breed that is sometimes timid with strangers and other dogs. It is affectionate with its owners and will tolerate older children provided there is no roughhousing. Training should be precise and patient. Socialization of the puppy is important and will help boost the confidence of this sensitive toy.

The Chinese Crested can be difficult to housebreak. It can also be a noisy breed. Spoiling may create a pushy, nippy dog that lacks confidence.

Both versions have the same behavioral profile. The Chinese Crested, particularly the hairless, is very susceptible to extremes in temperature and may need a sweater on a cold day. The hairless can also sunburn and may need sunblock on a bright summer day.

Best Home: An apartment is fine for this small breed. A walk or two each day will provide ample exercise. The owner of a Chinese Crested should be a patient, confident leader who desires an affectionate, busy, inquisitive dog. Spoiling may create a pushy, nippy dog that lacks confidence. Children are okay, but no roughhousing can occur. The elderly and the disabled make fine owners so long as they are able to train and socialize. Time to train and socialize must be available.

English Toy Spaniel

Origins: An old breed of Chinese or Japanese origin, the English Toy Spaniel was introduced into Spain and then England by traders in the sixteenth and seventeenth centuries.

Appearance: The English Toy Spaniel stands 9 to 10 inches at the shoulder and weighs 8 to 12 pounds. It has a small, compact body, a domed head, long ears, protruding eyes, and a docked tail. The shedding coat is long, silky, and wavy and requires regular brushing. It mats easily, particularly if the dog is left outside in wet weather. The Blenheim is red-and-white; the Prince Charles is white, black, and tan; and the Ruby is red.

Breed Profile: The English Toy Spaniel is a sweet, shy, easygoing toy that is quiet and affectionate with its owners and with those it is familiar with. Though initially timid, it quickly warms up to strangers and should be tolerant of older children provided no roughhousing is allowed.

Training should start early and should be patient and consistent. If pushed too hard, this breed will become passive-resistant, taking a head-in-the-sand attitude. Go slow, and socialize the dog from early on to increase its confidence. Spoiling may make the English Toy Spaniel pushy and will reduce its confidence.

This breed retains some spaniel instincts and may enjoy retrieving a ball or toy.

Housebreaking can be difficult with the English Toy Spaniel. Also, watch for ear infections and be aware that the protruding eyes can be easily damaged by rubbing against a wall or a leash. This breed is sensitive to extremes in temperature.

Best Home: An apartment is fine. One or two walks a day will provide ample exercise. The owner of an English Toy Spaniel should be a patient, calm leader who wants an easygoing lapdog. Spoilers may encourage bossy, nippy behavior. Nervous or overbearing types will reduce this breed's confidence level. Children should be fine provided no roughhousing occurs. The elderly and the disabled should do well with this breed if they can walk and socialize the dog.

Italian Greyhound

Origins: The smallest of the sighthounds, the Italian Greyhound is an ancient breed that appears in Greek and Turkish works of art that are 2000 years old. Once used as a ratter, it is now a companion dog.

Appearance: The Italian Greyhound stands 13 to 15 inches at the shoulder and weighs between 8 and 12 pounds. It is slender, fine-boned, and muscular and has a slightly curved back. The shedding coat is short, glossy, and low-maintenance, requiring only periodic brushing. The color may be blue, black, fawn, or reddish tan, with or without white markings.

Breed Profile: The Italian Greyhound is a high-strung friendly toy with lots of nervous energy. Though initially timid, it quickly warms up to strangers. It is an athletic dog that needs to run and play every day. Training should start early and must be patient and precise. Never be too hard on this sensitive breed. The Come and the Stay can be the most difficult commands to teach. Socialization is important and will help raise the dog's confidence level. Spoiling may create a pushy, nippy attitude.

Though not by nature aggressive, the Italian Greyhound may worry over the hectic unpredictability of young children and may bite if scared. No roughhousing should be allowed.

Housebreaking can be difficult with this breed. The Italian Greyhound is also very susceptible to the cold and may need a sweater on cool days. It has thin legs that could easily break if the dog jumps from a high place.

Best Home: An apartment is fine provided the dog gets out to run each day. The owner of an Italian Greyhound should be an active, patient leader who desires a high-energy, busy, affectionate toy dog. Spoilers and nervous types may encourage timid, nippy behavior. Older children are okay, provided they do not roughhouse. The elderly and the disabled can own this breed if they are able to socialize and exercise it.

Japanese Chin

Origins: Developed in China and introduced into Japan centuries ago, this companion to the nobility was brought to Europe in the nineteenth-century.

Appearance: The Japanese Chin stands 8 to 9 inches at the shoulder and weighs 6 to 8 pounds. It has a small, square body and a pushed-in, puggish face with

protruding eyes. The long, straight, silky coat does shed and requires a daily brushing and an occasional trim. The color may be black-and-white or red-and-white.

Breed Profile: This happy, playful, affectionate breed tends to be easy going but initially timid around strangers. The Japanese Chin can be mildly stubborn, but it usually responds to persistent, patient training. Socialization should start early, and will help build the confidence of this breed. The Japanese Chin may not tolerate the commotion caused by young children. Spoiling may create a dog that is controlling, nippy, and lacking in confidence.

The Japanese Chin may be difficult to housebreak, and can easily damage its protruding eyes on a door or a leash. It will sneeze and snore and may be susceptible to respiratory problems. It is also sensitive to extremes in temperature.

Best Home: An apartment is adequate for this easygoing breed, provided it is walked once or twice a day. The owner of a Japanese Chin should be an easygoing, patient leader who enjoys an affectionate, playful lapdog. Spoilers and nervous types could encourage pushy, nippy behavior. Older children are fine so long as they are not allowed to roughhouse. The elderly and the disabled make good owners if they can socialize and walk the dog.

Maltese

Origins: The Maltese was kept as a companion by the ancient Greeks and Romans, and also by the Phoenicians, who settled the island of Malta in 1500 B.C.

Appearance: The Maltese stands 7 to 8 inches at the shoulder and weighs between 4 and 6 pounds. It has a compact, petite body and a long, silky coat that sheds and must be brushed and combed every day. The coat is absorbent and must be kept dry to prevent mats. Many owners keep the coat in a short clip to reduce the amount of maintenance. The color is always white.

Breed Profile: The Maltese is a gentle, refined, sweet breed. Normally quiet and sensitive, it may be initially reserved with strangers. Though intelligent, it needs slow, patient training and should never be treated in an overbearing manner. Its tiny size and sensitive demeanor can cause it to worry when it is confronted with hectic, unpredictable activity. As a result, it may not tolerate small children. Socialization from puppyhood on will help boost this breed's confidence, as will avoidance of spoiling or coddling.

Because of its spaniel heritage, the Maltese may enjoy retrieving balls and other toys. This is an excellent exercise that will help build the dog's confidence.

The Maltese can be very difficult to housebreak and may be a picky eater. It is also sensitive to extremes in temperature.

Best Home: An apartment is fine for this small, quiet breed. A walk or some retrieving with a ball will provide adequate exercise. The owner of a Maltese should be a patient, easygoing leader who desires a sweet, lively little lapdog. The home environment should be free of hectic activity. Older children are fine provided no roughhousing occurs. Spoiling this breed may encourage bossy, nippy behavior and will lower the dog's confidence level. The elderly and the disabled make good owners if they can socialize and walk the dog. Time to groom this breed must be available.

Manchester Terrier, Toy

Origins: Developed in eighteenth- and nineteenth-century England, the Toy Manchester Terrier was used as a ratter and kept as a companion. Whippet and terrier bloodlines were crossed to produce this toy version of the Standard Manchester.

Appearance: The Toy Manchester Terrier stands 8 to 13 inches at the shoulder and weighs between 7 and 12 pounds. It has a small, muscular body, erect ears, and a short glossy, shedding coat that needs to be brushed only once a week. The color is always black-and-tan.

Breed Profile: The Toy Manchester Terrier has a similar behavioral profile to the Standard, with some minor differences. It is intelligent, high-strung, and very busy. Though affectionate with its owners, it can be suspicious of strangers. Often bossy, this breed needs early consistent, precise training and should not be spoiled. Being a terrier, this breed may show dog-aggression and will have a high prey drive toward small animals. The Toy Manchester may not tolerate the hectic activity of young children and may bite if provoked or worried.

This breed makes a good watchdog, but it may bark and dig incessantly if left in a yard for too long.

The Toy Manchester is harder to housebreak than the Standard and is also more sensitive to extremes in temperature. It may need a sweater on cold days.

Best Home: An apartment is fine, provided this breed is walked several times a day. The owner of a Toy Manchester Terrier should be an active, confident leader who desires a feisty, busy, intelligent toy. Older children who do not roughhouse are okay. Spoilers may create a bossy, nippy dog that lacks confidence. The elderly and the disabled can own this breed if they are able to train and walk it. There should be no small animals in the home. Time to socialize the dog must be available.

Miniature Pinscher

Origins: Miniature Pinschers have been around since the early nineteenth-century. Originally from Germany, Minpins are not scaled-down Dobermans but are actually a separate breed with terrier beginnings. Once used as ratters, they are now companion dogs.

Appearance: The Miniature Pinscher stands 10 to 12.5 inches at the shoulder and weighs 8 to 12 pounds. It has a compact, muscular body, cropped or uncropped ears, a docked tail, and a very short, glossy, shedding coat that requires almost no maintenance. The color may be reddish brown, black-and-rust, or chocolate.

Breed Profile: Someone forgot to tell this breed how small it is. The Minpin acts as if it weighs 110 pounds. Heaven help us if it did.

The Minpin is a high-strung, noisy, bellicose little devil that is actually much tougher in constitution than the Doberman Pinscher, which tends to be a much more sensitive dog.

The Miniature Pinscher's toughness is almost comical. We adopted one named Bo last year; he was extremely aggressive toward anyone or anything. It took us months just to get this little alligator to a manageable state. We seem to be the only ones who can own him and appreciate his angst.

Though Bo is an extreme case, The Minpin is by nature very stubborn and difficult to train. It has to be trained as if it were a big dominant dog, because that's what it thinks it is. Training must be firm and the trainer must have a no-nonsense attitude. This is a smart breed that will find ways to resist training.

This breed is suspicious of strangers and normally bonds to only one or two persons. It makes an excellent watchdog, can be quite dog-aggressive, and has a high prey drive toward small animals. If left in a yard, it may dig and bark.

This is not a good breed to own if you have children. It can be quite nippy and does not like excessive handling unless it chooses to be handled. It is also loud, making it a questionable choice for apartment-dwellers. This breed is personable, however, and can be a good companion if trained and socialized early on.

Like other toy dogs, the Minpin can be hard to house-train. Sensitive to extremes in temperature, it may need a sweater on cool days.

Best Home: An apartment is adequate, but keep in mind that this breed can be very noisy. If you are a strong-willed person without children, and if you want to take on a challenge, then one of these cantankerous little dogs might be an interesting choice. Do not spoil your Minpin, however, and do a finger count after each training session. The elderly and the disabled may have trouble controlling this dominant, temperamental breed. Time to train, socialize, and exercise this breed must be available.

Papillon

Origins: The Papillon was developed in France in the sixteenth-century. Its progenitors were small spaniel-type dogs. "Papillon" means "butterfly" in French, a suitable name for a breed whose ears look like butterfly wings. Once used as ratters, Papillons are now companion dogs.

Appearance: The Papillon stands 8 to 11 inches at the shoulder and weighs 6 to 10 pounds. Fine-boned yet robust, it has wide-set prick ears and a long, silky, shedding coat that requires a quick daily brushing.

Breed Profile: The Papillon is a happy, lively, affectionate little dog that warms up quickly to strangers. It accepts training more readily than other toys, perhaps because of its spaniel ancestry. It focuses well and can excel in the obedience ring. The Papillon makes a fun family pet and gets along well with children provided no roughhousing is permitted. Training should begin early and must be consistent and precise. Socialization will help raise the confidence level of this tiny breed. Spoiling will ellicit pushy behavior and will lower the dog's confidence.

Like the other toy dogs, a Papillon can get carried away with barking, especially when it grows suspicious of an unfamiliar sound or person. Tiny dogs feel they have to make up for their lack of size with a big mouth.

Because of its spaniel blood, the Papillon likes to retrieve balls and other toys. This is an excellent way to exercise the dog and build up its confidence.

Be careful with a Papillon around other dogs, particularly those from the Working Group and the Terrier Group; these little guys tend to look more like rodents or rabbits than dogs, and their appearance can bring out the prey drive in other breeds.

Housebreaking can be an issue with this breed, as it is with all toys. Also, remember the Papillon's delicate structure; it can easily break a leg while jumping off a table or chair. Don't let your children or your Golden Retriever play too roughly with a Papillon, for the same reason.

Though this breed is not as susceptible to the cold as other toys, you must remember that its small body mass cannot generate as much body heat, proportionately speaking, as can that of a larger dog; a sweater might be needed on a cold day.

Best Home: An apartment is fine, provided the dog is walked several times a day. The owner of a Papillon should be a consistent, patient leader who desires an active, playful, busy pet and not a couch potato. If you are looking for a small dog that can excel in the obedience ring, you should consider a Papillon.

Children are okay provided no roughhousing occurs. The Papillon is an excellent breed choice for the elderly and the disabled as long as they are physically able to walk it. Spoiling will elicit pushy behavior, however, and will lower the dog's confidence level.

Pekingese

Origins: An ancient Chinese breed, the Pekingese was brought back to Europe by English troops in the nineteenth-century. It has always been a companion dog.

Appearance: The Pekingese stands 8 to 9 inches at the shoulder and weighs between 10 and 14 pounds. It has a compact, sturdy, short-legged body, protruding eyes, and long ears. The shedding coat is long, straight, and dense with a thick under-coat. It needs to be brushed and combed every day and must be kept dry to prevent matting. Some owners prefer to keep the coat cut short to simplify maintenance. Colors include red, tan, fawn, black, black-and-tan, white, brindle, and particolor.

Breed Profile: From its inception, the Pekingese has been a pampered lapdog that fancies itself a tiny emperor. It has a controlling temperament and is not aware of the concept of owner dominance. This is one of the most difficult toys in terms of attitude. Pekingese are set in their ways and are very capable of biting if annoyed or pushed. This breed will often not cooperate during training; an owner must be persistent and patient. Spoiling will exaggerate the Pekingese's narcissistic nature and may result in aggression. This breed is almost never seen in the obedience ring, for good reason.

To be fair, much of this breed's snooty behavior comes from the tendency of owners to spoil them. Many owners treat a Pekingese as if it were their own human child, dressing it, fixing its hair, and letting it sit on the table during dinner.

The Pekingese is very suspicious of strangers and other dogs, and you should not consider this breed if you have children. Often noisy, it may dig if left in a yard. It is a good companion dog for the elderly and the disabled, however, because of its low exercise requirements and its tendency to bond closely to only one or two persons.

Housebreaking can be very difficult with a Pekingese. The breed can suffer from respiratory problems and is susceptible to ear infections and eye injuries. A Pekingese can also be sensitive to extremes in temperature and may be a picky eater.

Best Home: An apartment is fine; this breed needs only minimal exercise. The owner of a Pekingese should prefer a bossy, discriminating companion dog that likes to be pampered. Those who fancy this breed are quite likely to spoil it, but spoiling this inherently narcissistic breed will create a pushy dog that will bite if it feels so motivated. The Pekingese will not tolerate children. The elderly and the disabled may find this breed a welcome companion.

Pomeranian

Origins: A descendant of larger spitz-type sled dogs of Iceland, this vivacious toy was perfected in Pomerania, Germany, in the nineteenth-century.

Appearance: The Pomeranian stands 5 to 7 inches at the shoulder and weighs between 3 and 8 pounds. It has a tiny compact body and a long, coarse, shedding coat with a softer, insulative undercoat. A daily brushing is necessary to prevent matting. Colors include red, white, black, black-and-white, tan, beige, reddish brown, and particolor.

Breed Profile: The Pomeranian is a happy, spirited, intelligent breed. It is affectionate with its owners but can be initially reserved with strangers. Sassy and often stubborn, the Pomeranian needs consistent, patient training from puppyhood. It can actually be a good obedience dog if worked diligently. Socialization from puppyhood will help boost this small breed's confidence level. Spoiling will create a bossy, nippy dog that lacks confidence.

The Pomeranian is a good watchdog and can in fact be noisy. Though sometimes impertinent, it is much more willing to please than the Pekingese. It may not tolerate the antics of young children.

The Pomeranian is a difficult breed to housebreak, and it is sensitive to extremes in temperature.

Best Home: An apartment is fine for this breed. A walk each day is ample exercise. The owner of a Pomeranian should be a consistent, patient leader who desires a sassy, smart, active toy that can learn obedience well if properly trained. Spoilers and meek, nervous people may create a bossy, nippy dog that lacks confidence.

Older children are fine provided no roughhousing occurs. The elderly and the disabled make fine owners provided they can train and
walk the dog. Time to socialize this breed must also be available.

Poodle, Toy

Origins: Developed in Europe
centuries ago as a flusher and
retriever of birds, the Poodle
now comes in three sizes. The
Standard and Miniature are
listed in section 7: The Non-
Sporting Group. The Toy Poodle is discussed here.

Appearance: The Toy Poodle
stands under 10 inches at the
shoulder and weighs 5 to 8 pounds. It has a diminutive body and a
curly non-shedding coat that needs to be brushed twice a week
and clipped every two months. The English saddle clip and the
continental clip are high-maintenance styles used for show dogs.
The sporting clip is the easiest to maintain. In this style, the hair is
about an inch long on the body, with a pom-pom of longer hair
on the end of the tail, a topknot on the head, and a clean-shaven
face, feet, and tail. The coat color may be black, white, apricot,
gray, chocolate, or cream.

Breed Profile: The Toy Poodle is similar to the Miniature and the
Standard in temperament, albeit more lively and with more nervous
energy. It is an intelligent breed that is more suspicious of strangers
than its two brethren, and it may be timid if not socialized from puppyhood. The Toy Poodle becomes very attached to its owners and can
be a great obedience dog if trained with consistency and patience. If
spoiled, however, this breed easily becomes pushy, nippy, and timid. It
may not tolerate the unpredictability of young children.

Toy Poodles can be noisy, and make good watchdogs. House-breaking can be difficult with this breed; however, and it is prone to ear infections and extremes of temperature and may need a sweater on cold days.

Best Home: An apartment is fine for this breed. One or two walks a day will provide ample exercise. The owner of a Toy Poodle should be a consistent, patient leader who desires a lively toy dog that is capable of doing excellent work in obedience. Spoilers and meek types could elicit pushy, nippy behavior from this breed and will encourage timidity. Older children are fine provided no rough-housing occurs. The elderly and the disabled do well with this breed provided they are able to train and walk it. Time to socialize this breed should be available.

Pug

Origins: The Pug originated in Tibet in ancient times. In the sixteenth and seventeenth centuries, traders brought the breed to Europe, where it became a favorite companion of the aristocracy.

Appearance: The Pug stands 9 to 11 inches at the shoulder and weighs between 14 and 18 pounds. It has a solid, squarish body, a pushed-in muzzle, and protruding eyes. The shedding coat is coarse and short and needs to be brushed only once a week.

Breed Profile: The Pug is a happy, lovable dog with one of the sweetest dispositions of any breed. It is fun and playful, usually gets along with other dogs, and rarely shows aggression, making it a great family pet. Training can take some time because of its slightly stubborn nature, but the Pug usually comes around well if a patient, consistent technique is used. Socialization from puppyhood will increase this toy's confidence level. Spoiling may make this breed impertinent and timid.

A Pug usually warms up quickly to strangers. It will tolerate children, provided no roughhousing occurs. It makes a good apartment pet and is a good companion for the elderly and the disabled. It doesn't need a lot of exercise and is happy to be walked twice a day.

This breed can be difficult to housebreak and can develop sinus problems because of its blunt muzzle. It tends to wheeze and snore as well and is sensitive to extremes in temperature. This dog may need a sweater on a cold day. A Pug's eyes protrude slightly; you must be careful not to let the leash rub against them. This breed puts weight on easily, so do not overfeed the dog. Overall, however, this is one of the most congenial and adaptable breeds.

Best Home: An apartment is fine for this breed. A walk or two each day is sufficient exercise. The owner of a Pug should be a patient, easygoing leader who desires a sweet, affectionate toy dog as a companion. Spoilers may make this breed bossy and timid. Children are fine provided no roughhousing occurs. The elderly and the disabled do well with this breed so long as they are able to walk it. Time to socialize this breed should be available.

Shih Tzu

Origins: An ancient Chinese breed, the Shih Tzu may date back to the seventh century Tang dynasty. It has always been a companion dog.

Appearance: The Shih Tzu stands 8 to 11 inches at the shoulder and weighs between 10 and 16 pounds. It has a compact, sturdy body with short legs, a blunt muzzle, and a long, silky shedding coat that requires a daily brushing and combing. A lionlike mane radiates around the face. Periodic clipping is needed; Shih Tzus can be kept in a shorter clip to reduce maintenance. The color may be white-and-silver, white-and-black, and white-and-brown.

Breed Profile: The Shih Tzu is a feisty, playful, alert little breed that is affectionate with its owners and initially reserved with strangers. It is stubborn but not nearly as difficult as the Pekingese and the Lhasa Apso. Training should be consistent and patient. The Shih Tzu is intelligent and can be a good obedience dog if trained well. Spoiling may elicit pushy, nippy behavior and timidity. Socialization will increase confidence and should be started early. This dog may not tolerate young children.

The Shih Tzu may be difficult to housebreak and can be a picky eater. This breed can suffer from respiratory problems and may wheeze and snore. Its protruding eyes are susceptible to injury. The Shih Tzu normally does not have problems with extremes of temperature.

Best Home: An apartment is fine, provided the dog is walked several times a day. The owner of a Shih Tzu should be a patient, consistent leader who desires an active, curious breed. Spoilers and meek owners may elicit pushy, nippy behavior. Older children are fine provided no roughhousing occurs. The elderly and the disabled can own this breed if they are able to train and walk it. Time to groom and socialize must be made available.

Silky Terrier

Origins: A fairly recent creation, the Silky Terrier was developed in Australia by crossing the Australian Terrier with the Yorkshire Terrier. Once used as a ratter, it is now a companion dog.

Appearance: The Silky Terrier stands 8 to 10 inches at the shoulder and weighs 7 to 10 pounds. It is smaller than the Australian Terrier, but it's not considered frail. The coat is straight and glossy, sheds little, and needs to be brushed and combed periodically and given an occasional trim. The coat is always blue-and-tan.

Breed Profile: The Silky Terrier is an active, sweet, inquisitive breed with strong terrier roots. It is suspicious of strangers and makes a good watchdog. Initially resistant to training, the Silky needs firm yet patient training and early socialization. Spoiling may elicit pushy, nippy behavior and will reduce this breed's confidence level.

The Silky Terrier may show some dog-aggression and will have a high prey drive toward small animals. It may not tolerate young children. Housebreaking can be difficult. This breed may also be a barker and a digger.

Best Home: An apartment is fine, provided the dog is walked several times a day. The owner of a Silky Terrier should be a firm, patient leader who desires a lively, inquisitive, terrierlike toy that does not think of itself as a lapdog. Spoilers may elicit pushy, nippy behavior from this breed. Older children are acceptable so long as they are not allowed to roughhouse. The elderly and the disabled can do well with this breed if they are able to train and walk it. Time to socialize and groom this breed must be made available.

Yorkshire Terrier

Origins: Developed in England and Scotland in the nineteenth century, this terrier-toy was used by working people as a ratter. It is now exclusively a companion dog.

Appearance: The Yorkshire Terrier stands 7 to 9 inches at the shoulder and weighs 4 to 7 pounds. It has a compact, diminutive body and a long, silky shedding coat that mats easily and must be brushed and combed daily. It needs an occasional trim and can be kept in a shorter pet clip to lessen maintenance. The color may be blue-black or tan.

Breed Profile: Though developed from terrier bloodlines, this intelligent petite breed is less active and robust than its larger terrier cousins. It is affectionate with its owners but somewhat timid around strangers, preferring not to be petted by those it does not know. The Yorkie needs patient, consistent training and early socialization to combat a tendency toward timidity. Spoiling will lower this breed's confidence level and encourage nippy behavior.

The Yorkshire Terrier may be concerned about young children and dogs and may have a high prey drive toward smaller animals. It can be a barker and may dig if left alone in a yard. It needs little exercise to remain happy.

The Yorkshire Terrier can be extremely difficult to housebreak and may be a picky eater. It is also sensitive to extremes of temperature and may need a sweater on cold days.

Best Home: An apartment is fine for this breed. A walk each day will provide ample exercise. The owner of a Yorkshire Terrier should be a patient, consistent leader who desires a lively, affectionate, and somewhat discriminating companion. Spoilers and meek owners may elicit bossy, nippy behavior, and lower the dog's confidence. Older children are tolerable provided no roughhousing or hectic activity occurs. The elderly and the disabled make fine owners for this breed, given its low exercise requirement and its desire to bond closely with one or two persons. Time to socialize and groom the Yorkie should be made available.

The Non-Sporting Group

This group is a collection of dissimilar breeds that no longer have a clearly defined purpose other than that of providing companionship. None can easily be placed into any of the other groups. The Dalmatian is here, as is the Bulldog.

Bichon Frise

Origins: An old Mediterranean breed, the Bichon Frise was popular among Spanish sailors, who transported the dogs over their trade routes to the Canary Islands, Italy, France, and England. At first a pet of European aristocrats, the Bichon became a favorite of commoners in the nineteenth-century.

Appearance: The Bichon Frise stands 9 to 12 inches at the shoulder and weighs between 8 and 14 pounds. Its body is sturdier than that of the Toy Poodle. The non-shedding coat is puffy, curly, and coarser than the soft, thick undercoat. If not kept dry and brushed out, it will become matted and malodorous. A clip every two to three months is necessary.

Breed Profile: The Bichon Frise is a happy, lively, breed that is affectionate with its owners. It can be initially reserved with strangers, and may not tolerate the antics of small children. This intelligent though sometimes stubborn breed can excel in obedience if trained with patience and persistence. Though normally calm indoors, it can enjoy a game of fetch outside. If spoiled, the Bichon Frise can easily become pushy and nippy and may become timid. Its personality is similar to that of the Poodle, though this breed is slightly more discerning.

The Bichon Frise is a barker, and will make a good watchdog. If left in a yard, it may dig, and will certainly soil its high-maintenance coat. It is susceptible to ear infections and skin allergies and can be difficult to housebreak.

Best Home: An apartment is fine, provided the dog is walked twice a day. The owner of a Bichon Frise should be a consistent, patient leader who desires a lively, intelligent breed that excels in obedience if carefully taught. Older children should be okay if no roughhousing is allowed. The elderly and the disabled can do well with this breed, provided they are able to train and walk it. Time to socialize and groom this breed should be available.

Boston Terrier

Origins: Developed in nineteenth-century New England, the Boston Terrier was a result of crossing Bulldog and white English terrier bloodlines. It has always been a companion dog.

Appearance: The Boston Terrier stands 11 to 14 inches at the shoulder and weighs 15 to 20 pounds. It has a sturdy, muscular body, protruding eyes, a blunt muzzle, a docked tail, and a short, low-maintenance shedding coat that requires only periodic brushing. The color may be black or brindle with white markings.

Breed Profile: The Boston Terrier is a busy breed with lots of nervous energy. It bonds closely with its owners, but it can be more than a bit stubborn. Often suspicious of strangers, this breed may show some aggression toward other dogs and small animals. It will not tolerate the unpredictable behavior of young children. Training should begin early and be persistent but not overbearing. Socialization will increase its level of confidence, something most toys need. Spoiling may make this breed bossy, timid, and nippy and will encourage resistance to training. In extreme cases the dog may throw a tantrum during a training session.

The Boston can be noisy and may dig if left in a yard. It makes a good watchdog. The females are less noisy and dominant than the males.

The Boston likes to retrieve balls and other toys. This is a good constructive activity that will channel much of the dog's nervous energy.

Housebreaking can be difficult with this breed. Its protruding eyes are susceptible to injury from rubbing against a wall or a leash. The Boston is also susceptible to respiratory problems and may wheeze and snore. Extremes of temperature can also affect it; a sweater may be necessary on a cold day.

Best Home: An apartment is fine, provided the dog is walked twice a day. The owner of a Boston Terrier should be a patient leader who desires a lively, loyal companion. Older children who do not roughhouse should be okay. This breed can be a good pet for the elderly and the disabled if they are able to handle its high level of activity. Spoilers and meek owners may encourage stubborn, nippy behavior and will lower the dog's confidence level. Overbearing people may create fear-based aggression. Time to train, socialize, and walk the dog should be available.

Bulldog

Origins: First used in England during the Middle Ages as bait-ers and fighters of bulls, Bull-dogs were originally bred to have almost laughable courage and tenacity. These early dogs were incredibly aggressive. It wasn't until the nineteenth-century that the present per-sonable temperament was achieved.

Appearance: The Bulldog stands 13 to 15 inches at the shoulder and weighs between 40 and 60 pounds. It has a dense, powerful body, an extremely blunt muzzle, a pronounced underbite, and a short, smooth shedding coat that requires only a periodic brushing. The color may be brindle, white, fawn, red, or patched.

Breed Profile: The Bulldog is a sweet, stubborn, incredibly strong dog that, contrary to popular belief, is filled with athletic enthusi-asm. You haven't lived until you've called a Bulldog to you and watched this fifty-pound bowling ball of muscle build up momen-tum until it slams into you and knocks you across the room. It can't stop quickly once it gets going.

This is an extremely personable and loving breed, but because of its strength and enthusiasm, it is not always the best choice for the elderly or the disabled. Though normally not aggressive, it may resist training because it has a stubborn streak left over, no doubt, from its bull-fighting days.

The Bulldog needs training from early on, particularly in learning not to pull on the leash, not to jump up on people, and in general to contain its exuberance. It is normally good with kids and strangers; just make sure it does not get overenthusiastic and knock your friends or your children into next Tuesday with its bowling-ball body.

Training should start in puppyhood and should be firm and persistent. You must gain adequate control of this eager, powerful, stubborn breed early in the dog's life.

The Bulldog is susceptible to respiratory problems. It will snort and sneeze, spewing out—shall we say—undesirable secretions, usually while licking your face. The Bulldog also snores. In addition, the deep wrinkles on this dog's face and forehead tend to get infected if not cleaned and powdered with cornstarch once a day. Some Bulldogs may need eyelid surgery if a condition known as entropion sets in, causing the eyelids to turn in so that the eyelashes rub against the cornea. This breed is also sensitive to extremes in temperature and can easily become overheated. Finally, because the Bulldog is heavy for its frame, it can develop structural problems and arthritis later in life. Do not take this dog jogging or let it get overweight.

Best Home: An apartment is adequate provided this breed is exercised regularly. The owner of a Bulldog should be an active, capable leader who desires a sweet, personable, vigorous dog that is good with family and friends. Children are fine, but make sure that the dog does not bowl the little ones over during play, and never let play turn into roughhousing. The elderly and the disabled may have difficulty dealing with this breed's high level of enthusiasm; the Bulldog can be a very physical animal and, in its eagerness to play, may knock its owner down and cause an injury. Spoilers may increase this breed's level of obstinacy. Time to train and exercise this breed should be available.

Chinese Shar-Pei

Origins: An ancient breed, the Chinese Shar-Pei was revered by the nobility during the Han dynasty, around 200 B.C. The Shar-Pei and the Chow Chow are the only two breeds with a blue-black tongue; this may point to common ancestry. The Shar-Pei has been used as a fighting dog; its loose skin enables it to swing around and bite even while being bitten by another dog.

Appearance: The Shar-Pei stands 18 to 20 inches at the shoulder and weighs between 40 and 55 pounds. It has a medium-size muscular body, a fleshy face, a curled tail, and wrinkled skin on its face and body, though the wrinkles become less exaggerated as the dog matures. The shedding coat is short, harsh, and prickly to the touch and requires only periodic brushing. Coat length can vary from extremely short to just over an inch in length. The color may be black, chocolate, reddish brown, fawn, or cream.

Breed Profile: The Chinese Shar-Pei is an extremely dominant, controlling, moody breed that, though affectionate toward its owners, can be downright mean and dangerous. This breed has become very popular over the last decade and, like the Rottweiler and Cocker Spaniel, has suffered from poor breeding. It will bond with only one or two persons, it can be very suspicious of strangers, and it is likely to bite if approached or petted by anyone it does not know and respect. A Shar-Pei may not like being petted on the head even by its owner.

Definitely not a pet for families with children, the Shar-Pei is extremely territorial and dog-aggressive, and it excels as a watch dog. We know of several instances in which Shar-Peis have literally ripped another dog to shreds. This breed has a high prey drive toward small animals.

Training must start early and be uncompromisingly firm and consistent. This narcissistic breed can be wholly disobedient and defiant and will bite even its owner if so inclined. Tantrums and uncontrollable behavior often occur during training, particularly when the owner attempts to teach it to assume the Down position, a submissive posture that it hates. Socializing the puppy is mandatory and is the cornerstone of successfully owning this breed.

Under no circumstances should this breed be spoiled. Coddling will create a bossy, nasty, suspicious dog capable of seriously hurting someone.

The females tend to be less aggressive than the males. If you are considering a Shar-Pei, a female might be an intelligent option.

The Shar-Pei can suffer from hip dysplasia, entropion (a curling in of the eyelids), hypothyroidism (an underactive thyroid condition that can cause metabolic problems and panicky, stressful behavior), respiratory problems, and skin allergies. It drools and snorts and may snore.

We believe that those individuals currently breeding the Chinese Shar-Pei should take a long, hard look at the type of dog they are producing, and endeavor to breed a dog with a more stable, more predictable, less bellicose temperament.

Best Home: A house with a well-fenced secluded yard is essential. The owner of a Chinese Shar-Pei should be a strong, commanding no-nonsense leader who desires a protective, highly discriminating, territorial dog that will be at best reserved with strangers. The home should be quiet and predictable. Children will not be tolerated and could get badly hurt, particularly if roughhousing occurs. The elderly and the disabled should not consider this breed. Time to train, socialize, and exercise this breed must be available.

Chow Chow

Origins: The Chinese nobility once used this ancient breed for guarding and hunting. The Chow Chow's thick coat protected it in harsh weather and, unfortunately, provided clothing for the infamous Mongols, who also reportedly used Chows for food. No wonder they are such irritable, cranky dogs.

Appearance: The Chow Chow stands 16 to 20 inches at the shoulder and weighs between 50 and 65 pounds. It is a powerful medium-size dog with a short, broad muzzle. The coat may be rough or smooth. The rough coat is dense, straight, and coarse with a thick undercoat; it sheds profusely, particularly in early summer, and requires daily brushing. The smooth coat is shorter and less dense, but sheds just as much. The color may be red, blue, black, fawn, or cream.

Breed Profile: Not many people can successfully own a Chow Chow. Dogs of this breed tend to be very loyal to only one or two people. Intelligent and intensely stubborn, the Chow is highly resistant to training, particularly when learning the Down command. Proud and moody, this dog likes to take the lead and have its own way. It does not like to be touched on the head, legs, or feet, even by its owner, and can be a nightmare to groom.

The Chow is extremely aloof with strangers and can be vicious, even to family members. It will not tolerate lots of people coming and going and prefers a consistent, predictable environment. It can be very dog-aggressive and has a high prey drive toward small animals. The Chow may bite a stranger who reaches out to pet it. And forget about allowing any children around a Chow.

Training must begin early and must be firm and persistent. This breed despises the very idea of submitting to anyone and may attempt to bite even its owner if so inclined. Socialization is mandatory and will be the cornerstone of successful ownership of a Chow. Spoiling a Chow will create a bossy, dangerous animal.

As a Chow owner you will very likely have to deal with challenges to your authority, and you will probably face some aggression problems with this breed, no matter how effective a leader you are.

The Chow needs regular exercise each day to stay healthy. It is susceptible to hip dysplasia, entropion (a curling in of the eyelids), and skin disorders, and it does not do well in warm climates.

Best Home: A house with a well-fenced, secluded yard is essential. If you lead a predictable, quiet life, are a no-nonsense owner with strong leadership skills, and prefer an aloof, protective, serious dog, then this might be your breed. Chows are not advisable for those who have children. The elderly and the disabled may not be able to establish dominance with a Chow and should consider another breed. There should be no other small animals in the home. Spoilers may create a dominant, dangerous animal that bites. Time to train and socialize this breed must be made available.

Dalmatian

Origins: Known for its role as a carriage and fire engine dog, the Dalmatian has historically had a calming effect on horses; its attractive appearance also enhanced the prestige of the carriages of aristocrats as they sped through the streets of Europe during the nineteenth-century.

Appearance: The Dalmatian stands 19 to 23 inches at the shoulder and weighs between 40 and 60 pounds. Its sleek, muscular body resembles that of a small pointer. The smooth, short, shedding coat is easily maintained by brushing once a week. The color is white with either black or liver spots, preferably about the size of a quarter. Puppies are born all white and develop spots in a few weeks.

Breed Profile: Forget the movie. The Dalmatian is not always the lovable, endearing dog of Disney fame. It can suffer from more behavioral and physiological problems than most breeds.

Active and filled with nervous energy, the Dalmatian is a slow learner and is easily distracted, partly because of its powerful sense of smell. When put into a new situation or stressed in any way, it may internalize the stress and become passive-resistant, taking a head-in-the-sand attitude. This, combined with the breed's stubborn nature, makes the Dalmatian unpredictable and difficult to train.

The Dalmatian bonds very closely with its owner and, even more than the German Shepherd, exhibits profound separation anxiety, particularly when kenneled for a long time. It often does not eat well when kenneled and it tends to lose weight. When left at home alone, this breed can be destructive. Though close to its owner, the Dalmatian has a very low desire to please, unlike the retrievers and the German Shepherd.

This breed needs a predictable, stable environment and does not do well around young children. It is suspicious of strangers and, when worried or resistant, may bite. Strangers should not be allowed to reach down and pet a Dalmatian.

Training must begin early and must never be overbearing or rushed. You must make very clear just what you want from a Dalmatian, or you will risk stressing the dog. Socialization is important as well, and should begin in puppyhood.

On the positive side, the Dalmatian can make a good bird dog, and it excels as a jogging partner because of its trim, muscular build.

In our experience, about one out of five Dalmatians has some degree of hearing loss. In fact, we regularly get Dalmatians in for training that are totally deaf. Much of the time the owners don't even know this; they think the dog is just stubborn. Deafness is commonly overlooked in puppies, and it is a problem that breeders need to work hard to eliminate.

This breed can also suffer from hypothyroidism and ear infections. Skin problems are common in Dalmatians, as are allergies. These dogs may develop lick sores on their front feet, resulting from a nervous reaction to stress. The tips of their ears sometimes become raw and bloody as a result of the Dalmatian's habit of shaking its head vigorously, a movement that may be caused by ear problems. The Dalmatian can also suffer from urinary tract infections and can be difficult to housebreak.

Best Home: A house with a fenced yard is essential. The owner of a Dalmatian should be a consistent leader who desires a sensitive, highly active dog rather than a couch potato. Older children are okay, provided they participate in the training and do not roughhouse. The Dalmatian may be too active a breed for the elderly and the disabled. Spoilers may elicit pushy, nippy behavior and will lower the dog's confidence level, thereby encouraging timidity. Overbearing types may encourage fear-based aggression. The Dalmatian should be exercised regularly in order to help focus its energy. Time to train, socialize, and exercise should be made available.

Finnish Spitz

Origins: Developed centuries ago in Finland, this breed was used to alert the hunter to the location of birds by barking and yodeling. It is said that the dog would slowly wave its tail to capture and hold the bird's attention while waiting for the arrival of the hunter.

Appearance: The Finnish Spitz
stands 15 to 20 inches at the shoulder and weighs between 25 and

35 pounds. It has a sturdy medium-size body with a coyote-like face and a curled tail. The shedding coat is long, hard, and straight with a thick undercoat. Regular brushing is required. The color is golden red, sometimes with white markings on the chest and feet.

Breed Profile: Intelligent, lively, and independent, this northern breed is affectionate with its owners and initially suspicious of strangers. It may not appreciate the busy nature of little children.

Like the other northern breeds, the Finnish Spitz is stubborn and can be difficult to train, partly because it was bred to function independently of the hunter. Training should be consistent and firm but not overbearing. The most difficult command to teach, as with all northern breeds, is the Come. Socialization is important and should begin in puppyhood. Spoiling may encourage impertinent, nippy behavior.

The Finnish Spitz has a high prey drive and may be dog-aggressive. It is also very noisy and will bark incessantly. It is a clean dog that rarely gives off odors.

Best Home: An apartment is adequate provided the dog is exercised daily. Bear in mind, however, that this breed barks a lot. The owner of a Finnish Spitz should be a consistent leader who desires an intelligent, independent dog. Older children are fine provided no roughhousing occurs. The elderly and the disabled can own this dog if they are able to train and exercise it. Spoilers may encourage impertinence and nippy behavior. Time to train, socialize, and exercise the dog should be made available.

French Bulldog

Origins: Developed in England and France during the nineteenth century, this breed was the result of a cross between the toy English bulldog and various other breeds. It has always been primarily a companion dog.

Appearance: The French Bulldog stands 10 to 12 inches at the shoulder and weighs between 18 and 28 pounds. It has a compact, muscular body, batlike ears, and a straight or screwed tail. The short, smooth shedding coat requires only periodic brushing. The color may be white, brindle, fawn, or brindle-and-white.

Breed Profile: The French Bulldog is a happy, gregarious, affectionate breed that is initially reserved with strangers but warms up to them quickly. Though mildly stubborn, it responds well to patient, consistent training techniques. Spoiling may increase its stubborn nature. It is a relatively quiet, clean little dog that can get by with minimal exercise.

The French Bulldog normally gets along well with children. It will tolerate other dogs and can even enjoy the company of cats. It is a superb companion dog.

This breed can be difficult to housebreak and may suffer from respiratory problems. Care must be taken to protect its protruding eyes. It does not cope well with extremes in temperature, and it may wheeze and snore.

Best Home: An apartment is fine for this breed. One or two walks each day will provide ample exercise. The owner of a French Bulldog should be a patient, easygoing leader who enjoys an affectionate, playful companion. Children are fine so long as no rough-housing occurs. Spoilers could create a stubborn, bossy attitude in the dog and may lower its confidence level. The elderly and the disabled do well with this breed if they are able to train and walk it. Time to train and socialize should be available.

Keeshond

Origins: Developed in six-teenth-century Holland, the Keeshond served as a watchdog on barges. Pomeranian, Samo-yed, and Norwegian Elkhound bloodlines were crossed to pro-duce this breed.

Appearance: The Keeshond stands 16 to 18 inches at the shoulder and weighs between 35 and 42 pounds. It has a sturdy medium-sized body, a pretty fox-like face, a curled tail, and a full, straight, coarse coat with a dense, soft undercoat. A mane of hair surrounds the neck. Shedding is year-round; a daily brushing is helpful. The Keeshond's coat is unique in that many of the overcoat hairs are either black-tipped or silvery.

Breed Profile: The Keeshond is a pretty, lively, intelligent breed with lots of nervous energy. Though friendly, it can be initially re-served with strangers. Training should be persistent, precise, and never overbearing. The Keeshond is a northern breed and has an independent mind-set. The Come command may be the most dif-ficult to teach. Spoiling may encourage bossy, nippy behavior and may elicit a timid, fearful attitude in the dog. Socialization should begin early and will help increase confidence. When properly trained, this breed can excel in obedience competition.

The Keeshond can be a barker and may be destructive if left alone for long periods. It is an active breed that requires daily exercise; it can be taught to retrieve and can enjoy learning to run an agility course. Grooming can be time-consuming, but should be done regularly.

The Keeshond may be susceptible to hypothyroidism and skin allergies. It does not do well in warm climates.

Best Home: An apartment is adequate, provided the dog is exercised daily. Keep in mind, however, that this breed can be a barker. The owner of a Keeshond should be a consistent, confident leader who desires an active, busy breed capable of learning a lot. Those who want a quiet, lazy breed should look elsewhere. Spoilers and nervous owners may encourage pushy or timid behavior. Overbearing owners may create fear-based aggression in the dog. Children who do not roughhouse are fine. The elderly and the disabled can own this breed, provided they are able to train and exercise it. Time to train, socialize, and exercise the dog should be available.

Lhasa Apso

Origins: An ancient Tibetan breed, the Lhasa Apso was first used as a watchdog and was known as the Bark Lion Sentinel Dog. Its job was to alert large mastiff-type dogs to the approach of strangers. The long coat was developed to help insulate the Lhasa against the cold Tibetan weather. Today it is a companion dog.

Appearance: The Lhasa Apso stands 9 to 11 inches at the shoulder and weighs between 12 and 15 pounds. Its sturdy body is long and low. It has a short muzzle, protruding eyes, and a long, straight, absorbent coat that sheds and will become malodorous if not kept dry. Daily brushing and combing are required to prevent matting. A shorter pet clip is easier to maintain and is a popular among Lhasa owners. The colors may be white, black, reddish brown, cream, gray, or particolor.

Breed Profile: The Lhasa Apso is a willful, discriminating, independent breed that can be downright nasty at times. It is a consummate watchdog and can be very suspicious of strangers. Having been pampered for centuries, this breed has developed a dominant, narcissistic attitude that makes it very difficult to train. A firm, consistent, patient training technique is necessary from the start; you must clearly establish your dominance if you want to live with a Lhasa. Tantrums and aggressive feints are common tactics that the Lhasa uses to avoid learning or obeying a command. If spoiled, this breed will take over the household and become bossy, nippy, and extremely antisocial. It bonds closely to only one or two persons; we have known Lhasas that preferred one spouse to the other and would not allow the less favorite one to sleep in the same bed with the other.

Socialization is essential from puppyhood to prevent territorial aggression. The females tend to be less prone to nastiness and may be easier to train. The Lhasa will not tolerate children whom it sees as competitors for attention, and no roughhousing should ever be permitted.

The Lhasa Apso is susceptible to respiratory problems and injuries to its protruding eyes. It also wheezes and snores.

Pick a Lhasa puppy carefully. Try to spend time with the parents and the litter.

Best Home: An apartment is fine provided the dog is walked daily. Keep in mind, though, that Lhasas may bark a lot. The owner of a Lhasa Apso should be a competent leader who desires a discriminating, vain companion dog. We have seen owners who treat their Lhasas as if they were human; if you do this, you will have to organize your life around the dog, and it will become a tyrant. Spoiling will accentuate this breed's propensity to be bossy, nippy, and antisocial.

The Lhasa Apso does not easily tolerate children and may bite at the onset of roughhousing. The elderly and the disabled can own this breed if they are able to train and walk it; realize, however, that this breed is attuned to weakness, be it physical or behavioral, and will increase its dominant, bossy behavior accordingly.

Do not keep a Lhasa in a yard for long periods; it may bark incessantly and become a matted, smelly mess. Time to train, groom, and walk this dog must be available.

Poodle, Standard and Miniature

Origins: Originally bred in medieval Europe as retrievers and flushers of birds, Poodles are now companion dogs. The Standard Poodle and the Miniature Poodle are both in the Non-Sporting Group; the Toy Poodle is described in Chapter 6: The Toy Group.

Appearance: The Standard Poodle stands 15 inches or taller at the shoulder and weighs 50 to 65 pounds. The Miniature stands 10 to 15 inches at the shoulder and weighs between 15 and 35 pounds. In both varieties the coat is curly and non-shedding and needs to be clipped every two months. The English saddle clip and the continental

clip are high-maintenance show cuts. The sporting clip is easiest to maintain. In this style the hair on the body is about an inch long, there is a pom-pom on the tip of the tail, a topknot of hair remains on the head, and the face, feet, and tail are clean-shaven. The colors may be black, white, apricot, gray, chocolate, or cream.

Breed Profile: Both varieties are intelligent, alert, agile dogs that are normally friendly and eager to please. They accept people outside of the family, and yet they make effective watchdogs. Their bouncy enthusiasm is endearing, but it sometimes gets them into trouble. The Poodle's high level of energy is not for those who seek a lazy, easygoing dog. Both varieties, but especially the Standard, need daily exercise. Retrieving is a constructive, enjoyable exercise in which they can excel.

Poodles learn quickly. Many are seen in the obedience ring and in agility competitions. They will respond well to training as long as you avoid heavy-handed techniques. The Miniature tends to be a bit more high-strung and nervous, a trait that escalate into fear-based aggression and biting if the dog feels threatened. The Miniature is more likely to bite simply because it gets pampered and spoiled more often than the Standard. The Standard can be one of the best family dogs around and can get along wonderfully with children.

Again, Poodles need regular clipping, so do your groomer a favor and begin handling, nail-clipping, and brushing sessions early in the dog's life.

Best Home: A home with a fenced yard is preferable for the Standard but is not essential for the Miniature. The owner of either variety should be a patient, consistent leader who prefers a smart, happy, energetic dog capable of excelling in obedience. Both breeds are very light on their feet and therefore make good jogging partners. Both varieties enjoy the company of children, though the Standard may be able to deal with their youthful antics better than the Miniature. Spoiling these dogs could encourage stubborn, nippy behavior, particularly in the Miniature. The elderly and the disabled do well with the Miniature, provided they are able to train and walk it. The Standard may be too big and too active for them. Time to train and exercise these breeds should be available.

Schipperke

Origins: Developed in Belgium during the seventeenth and eighteenth centuries, this breed may have been developed by crossing larger black sheepdog breeds with a northern breed such as the Keeshond. It was used as a watchdog on canal boats and as a ratter. Today it is primarily a companion dog.

Appearance: The Schipperke stands 10 to 13 inches at the shoulder and weighs between 12 and 18 pounds. Its body is sturdy and compact. It has no tail. The face has a foxlike quality to it. The shedding coat is short on the face, ears, and legs and straight, thick, and hard on the body. The undercoat is dense and soft. Regular brushing is helpful. The color is black.

Breed Profile: The Schipperke is an active, spirited, courageous breed that is a natural watchdog. It is intelligent, independent, and suspicious of strangers. Training can be challenging with this headstrong, curious breed, and the trainer needs to be persistent and firm without being overbearing. If annoyed or pushed too hard, the Schipperke may bite. Socialization from puppyhood will increase its trust and confidence. Spoiling may encourage bossy, nippy behavior and timidity.

The Schipperke can be dog-aggressive and has a high prey drive toward small animals. It is a noisy breed and may become restless and destructive if left alone too long. Housebreaking can also be difficult. The Come command can be difficult to teach this headstrong breed.

Best Home: An apartment is adequate if the dog is exercised daily, but bear in mind that this breed barks a lot. The owner of a Schipperke should be a competent leader who desires a busy, curious breed that is a natural watchdog. Those who desire a quiet lapdog should look elsewhere. Spoiling may encourage bossy, nippy behavior and will accentuate this breed's distrust of strangers. Overbearing people may encourage fear-based aggression. Older children who participate in the training process are okay, but no roughhousing should be allowed. The elderly and the disabled can own this breed if they can train and walk it. Time to train, socialize, and exercise should be available.

Shiba Inu

Origins: An old Japanese breed, the Shiba Inu was originally used as a hunting dog. Today it is considered a companion. It is currently being admitted into the AKC registry.

Appearance: The Shiba Inu stands 13 to 16 inches at the shoulder and weighs between 15 and 30 pounds. It has a plush, shedding coat that requires regular brushing. The color may be red, red-and-black, or black. Tan or white markings are common.

Breed Profile: The Shiba Inu is a lively, independent breed. Though affectionate with its owners, it can be initially reserved with strangers. It tends to be stubborn with regard to training; a precise, patient technique should be used. Like other northern breeds, the Shiba is not very trustworthy off-leash, and probably will not come when called unless this command is taught from a young age and practiced regularly.

A relatively clean, quiet animal, the Shiba makes a good apartment pet, but will need daily exercise. This breed has a higher than normal prey drive toward small animals. Children are okay provided they do not roughhouse or tease.

Best Home: The Shiba Inu can live in an apartment provided it is regularly walked. The owner should be a calm leader who desires a sometimes discriminating and slightly willful dog that keeps clean and quiet. The elderly or disabled can own a Shiba provided they can walk and train it.

Tibetan Spaniel

Origins: An ancient Tibetan companion and watchdog, this breed was developed with good vision and a loud bark, to enable it to alert huge Mastiffs to a wolf intrusion into the sheep herd or to the approach of visitors.

Appearance: The Tibetan Spaniel stands 9 to 10 inches at the shoulder and weighs between 9 and 15 pounds. It has a long, low body, a domed head with a short muzzle, and a long, silky shedding coat with an undercoat that grows through the outer coat. A long mane of hair surrounds the neck. The color may be white, black, black-and-tan, fawn, reddish brown, or cream.

Breed Profile: An alert, busy, observant breed, the Tibetan Spaniel is affectionate with its owners and suspicious of strangers. Often stubborn, it can be an uncooperative obedience student. If spoiled, it can be nippy and controlling. Patient, persistent training should begin early and should include as much socialization as possible to reduce this breed's suspicious nature.

The Tibetan Spaniel is a good watchdog and companion. It may not tolerate the unpredictable activities of small children. No roughhousing should be allowed.

Housebreaking can be difficult with this breed. The Tibetan Spaniel wheezes, is susceptible to respiratory problems, and may overheat easily.

Best Home: An apartment is fine for this breed, but potential owners should be aware that these dogs do bark a lot. A daily walk is ample exercise. The owner of a Tibetan Spaniel should be a patient, persistent leader who desires a busy, alert, watchful companion. Older children are fine so long as no roughhousing occurs. This breed makes a fine pet for the elderly and the disabled if they are able to walk it. Time to train and socialize this breed should be available.

Tibetan Terrier

Origins: This ancient Tibetan dog is not a true terrier at all, though its size and coat may give that impression. Always a companion, this breed was often given to visitors as a good-luck charm. The bloodlines of the Tibetan Terrier remained pure for centuries because of the remoteness of its homeland.

Appearance: A sturdy medium-size dog, the Tibetan Terrier stands 14 to 17 inches at the shoulder and weighs between 18 and 30 pounds. Its feet are large for its size, a result of its having evolved in a snowy country. The shedding coat is long and slightly wavy, with a softer, absorbent undercoat. It must be brushed and combed daily to prevent matting. The coat can be kept in a shorter pet clip to reduce maintenance. The color may be white, black, gray, tan, or patched.

Breed Profile: Happy, friendly, and playful, the Tibetan Terrier is not a bossy or dominant breed. It is initially reserved with strangers, but it usually warms up quickly. Though active, it tends to be a quiet, thoughtful breed that responds well to patient, precise training.

Spoiling may create control problems and will encourage timidity. Overbearing techniques may elicit fear-biting. Socialization, begun early, will help reduce timidity and increase confidence.

The Tibetan Terrier is normally good with children and usually gets along well with other animals.

Housebreaking can be difficult with this breed. Its long ears should be cleaned regularly.

Best Home: An apartment is adequate if the dog is exercised. The owner of a Tibetan Terrier should be a patient, easygoing leader who desires an active, sensitive, thoughtful companion. Nervous or spoiling types will reduce this breed's confidence level. Children are fine provided no roughhousing occurs. The elderly and the disabled can own this breed if they are able to walk it. Time to train, exercise, and groom this breed should be available.

The Herding Group

Many people believe that the Herding Group contains the most intelligent breeds. These medium-size, athletic dogs have served for thousands of years as herders of sheep, cattle, and other domesticated animals. They also make admirable house pets and great obedience dogs.

Australian Cattle Dog

Origins: The Australian Cattle Dog played a vital role in the colonization of a continent. During the nineteenth century Australian cattle ranchers had a problem: grazing areas were immense, and consequently their stock would disperse and become almost feral. Traditional herding dogs were not tough enough to deal with the vast expanses, the heat, and the wild unruly cattle. The Australian Cattle Dog was developed by crossing the wild dingo with a Smooth Collie–type herding dog from Great Britain. The result was a quiet, hardy, strong, intelligent dog with incredible stamina, courage, and drive. This is one tough breed.

Appearance: The Australian Cattle Dog stands 17 to 20 inches at the shoulder and weighs between 35 and 45 pounds. It has a strong medium-size body and a short weather-resistant shedding outer coat with a dense undercoat. The color may be a mottled blue, white, and gray or a speckled red-and-white.

Breed Profile: The Australian Cattle Dog might as well be ten feet tall and weigh three tons. It was bred to be a tough little dynamo, and for most owners it would not make a good pet. It takes a strong, diligent leader to live with a Cattle Dog. This breed needs to work. It can be very suspicious of strangers, and it can become aggressive without warning. Though it will be loyal and loving to your family and protective of your children, it will not deal well with your children's friends. It may interpret playful wrestling and chase games as a threat or as a call to herd. Trouble will ensue, especially if the child or adult in question begins to scream and run. If allowed to roam, a dog of this breed will take over a neighborhood, chasing anything in sight, including Buicks on the Interstate.

This breed needs firm obedience training. From the moment the puppy comes home, it needs structure and constant socialization to reduce the possibility of aggression problems later on. If you are a softy, forget about this breed. This is an admirable breed, but it will be too much for most owners. If you have children, if you are nurturing and easygoing, or if you don't have lots of time, then pass on this breed.

The Australian Cattle Dog may be susceptible to hip dysplasia.

Best Home: A house with a fenced yard is essential. The owner of an Australian Cattle Dog must be a no-nonsense leader who desires an active, hardworking, driven breed and who is naturally capable of establishing and maintaining dominance. A working cattle or sheep ranch would be an excellent home for this breed. Easygoing, meek, and spoiling types will create a dominant, aggressive animal capable of biting and of harassing the neighbors. Only mature older children capable of working the dog in obedience are acceptable. The elderly and the disabled should not consider this breed. Time to train, socialize, and work this breed on herding, in agility, or in some other constructive exercise must be available.

Australian Shepherd

Origins: The result of crossing numerous medium-size European and Australian herding breeds, this smart, energetic working dog has won favor worldwide as a masterful herder of sheep.

Appearance: The Australian Shepherd stands 18 to 23 inches at the shoulder and weighs between 45 and 60 pounds. It has an athletic medium-size body and a medium-length shedding coat that can be wavy or straight. Regular brushing is necessary. The color may be blue merle (mottled black, blue, and gray), red merle (intermixed red and white speckles), red, or black. All coat colors can have white or light brown patches.

Breed Profile: The Australian Shepherd is an extremely intelligent and active breed. For most of its existence, it has been bred specifically to be a high-energy herder and not a house pet. Recently, however, a less high-strung show type has been produced. This show type is a much more desirable pet for a family than is the traditional working Australian Shepherd, which tends to be skittish and very active. Die-hard Aussie aficionados have balked at this toned-down show type, claiming that it will reduce the herding abilities of the breed. We feel that this version is much more controllable and confident in a family environment than is the working variety.

Though often initially resistant to training, the Aussie can excel at competition obedience, agility, and almost any task you put to it. Retrieving or catching a Frisbee will keep this breed happy and occupied.

Though intelligent and affectionate with its owner, it can be suspicious of strangers, and the Australian Shepherd may want to chase cars, bikes, joggers, and small children. If kept too long by itself, it may become noisy and destructive. Providing the dog with firm, consistent leadership and challenging, interesting tasks will ensure successful ownership. Submissive and permissive owners may get walked over by this sometimes impetuous breed.

The Australian Shepherd can be susceptible to hip dysplasia and eye problems. The blue merle dogs can be susceptible to deafness.

Best Home: A house with a fenced yard is essential. The owner of an Australian Shepherd should be a firm, consistent, active leader who desires an extremely intelligent, active dog capable of learning a lot. Older children should be okay provided no roughhousing occurs. Placating or meek owners may not be able to control this breed. The elderly and the disabled should consider a less active breed. Time to exercise and obedience-train the dog must be available.

Bearded Collie

Origins: Developed in seventeenth- and eighteenth-century England and Scotland, this breed was used for herding and cattle droving. Its weather-resistant coat enables it to withstand harsh, wet climates.

Appearance: The Bearded Collie stands 20 to 22 inches at the shoulder and weighs between 45 and 55 pounds. It has an athletic medium-size body and a long, flat, shaggy, shedding coat that mats easily and absorbs odors, making a daily brushing and combing essential. The coat can be kept in a shorter clip to reduce maintenance. The coat may be black or blue-gray with or without white, it may be or fawn or brown, both with or without white. The color may lighten or darken as the dog ages.

Breed Profile: Active, playful, and friendly, the Bearded Collie is initially reserved with strangers, but it comes around quickly. This is an intelligent, sensitive, and mildly stubborn breed that responds well to consistent training if the technique is firm but not over-bearing. The Come command can be the hardest to teach.

The Bearded Collie, like most other herding breeds, may want to chase cars, bikes, and joggers. Though good with children, it may chase them and nip at their heels. Children should not be allowed to play chase games with this breed.

The Bearded Collie needs regular exercise. It can excel at competition obedience, agility work, and herding.

Best Home: A house with a fenced yard is essential. The owner of a Bearded Collie should be a consistent leader who desires an enthusiastic, friendly family dog that can excel in obedience work. Children are fine, provided no chasing or roughhousing is permitted. Spoilers and nervous owners may reduce the dog's confidence and promote timidity and fear-biting. The elderly and the disabled may have trouble owning this active breed. Time to train, exercise, socialize, and groom the Bearded Collie must be available.

Belgian Malinois, Belgian Sheepdog, and Belgian Tervuren

Origins: Developed in Belgium during the nineteenth century, these three similar breeds were bred for versatility. They excel at herding, tracking, police, military, and search-and-rescue work.

Appearance: All three breeds stand 22 to 26 inches at the shoulder and weigh between 55 and 80 pounds. The Malinois tends to be on average slightly heavier, the Tervuren slightly lighter, the Sheepdog in between. All three have large, muscular, athletic bodies. The shedding coat of the Malinois is short and straight, with a soft undercoat; it needs to be brushed once a week. It is fawn-colored with black-tipped hairs. Its mask is black. The shedding coat of the Sheepdog is black, medium-long, straight, and full, with a soft undercoat; it must be brushed several times a week. The shedding coat of the Tervuren is the same as the Sheepdog, but it is fawn-colored with black-tipped hairs and a black mask.

Breed Profile: All three breeds are active, intelligent, and territorial. Though somewhat similar to the German Shepherd in physique, the Belgians tend to be more sensitive and slightly less gregarious. Suspicious of strangers, they make good watchdogs and are protective of home and property. They are good with their owners' children, but may not tolerate visiting children who run about or roughhouse with them or with family members.

Training and socialization should begin early for these three breeds, and should be persistent, patient, and never overbearing. If pushed too hard, these dogs may become passive-resistant, (taking a head-in-the-sand attitude). Spoiling may create stubborn, nippy, timid behavior. Overbearing techniques may encourage fear-biting.

All three may want to chase cars, bikes, and joggers and may chase children and nip at their heels. No chase games should be played with any of these three.

The Malinois tends to be slightly more outgoing and stubborn than the other two. The Tervuren tends to be slightly more sensitive and reserved; the Sheepdog falls somewhere in between.

In all three breeds, there is a relatively small concern with regard to hip dysplasia.

Best Home: A house with a fenced yard is essential for all three breeds. The owner of a Belgian Malinois, Sheepdog, or Tervuren should be a firm, patient, thoughtful leader who is never nervous, overbearing, or placating and who desires an active, intelligent, and somewhat discriminating and protective dog. The Malinois may need a firmer training style. All three breeds need regular exercise and should be given a constructive job to do, such as competition obedience, herding, or tracking. Children are okay provided no roughhousing or chase games occur. The elderly and the disabled can own these dogs provided they are able to obedience-train and exercise them. Time to train, exercise, and socialize these breeds must be available.

Bouvier des Flandres

Origins: Developed in Belgium in the nineteenth century, this working breed excels at herding, herd-guarding, and cart pulling. It has also been used for tracking by the police and military.

Appearance: The Bouvier des Flandres stands 23.5 to 27.5 inches at the shoulder and weighs between 65 and 95 pounds. Its body is large, powerful, and thick-boned. The tail is docked. The shedding coat is weather-resistant, shaggy, and somewhat harsh, with a soft undercoat. The dog has a beard, a mustache, and bushy eyebrows. Daily brushing is needed to prevent matting, and the dog should be clipped every three or four months. Show dogs must be hand-stripped to preserve the texture and luster of the coat. The coat can be kept in a shorter clip to facilitate maintenance. The color may be black, salt-and-pepper, gray, brindle, or fawn.

Breed Profile: Easygoing but aloof, this breed tends to be moody and serious. Though affectionate with its owners, the Bouvier is very suspicious of strangers and will serve well as a watchdog for your home and property. Training can be difficult due to its stubborn, dominant nature. Passive resistance is common, and aggression is possible when the dog is annoyed or threatened. Training should be patient and firm but not overbearing. The Bouvier learns slowly and can be defiant. The Down and the Come can be the hardest commands to teach this controlling breed.

The Bouvier has a high prey drive and may be very dog-aggressive. It may want to chase cars, joggers, and bikes. Though normally good with its own family's children, it may be intolerant of visiting children, especially if they are running around. No roughhousing or chasing should be tolerated. Spoiling can encourage dominant, controlling, nippy behavior in this breed, and may promote timidity. Overbearing training techniques may elicit fear-biting. Confident, firm leadership and early socialization are crucial to successfully owning a Bouvier.

The Bouvier needs daily exercise. It tends to bark and may be destructive and noisy if left alone too long. It is susceptible to hip dysplasia and bloat.

Best Home: A house with a fenced yard is essential. The owner of a Bouvier des Flandres should be a firm, strong, active leader who desires a reserved, protective dog. Mild, placating, or nervous owners may have trouble establishing dominance over this breed. Older children who take part in the training process are fine, provided no roughhousing or chasing is permitted. The elderly and the disabled may have a hard time establishing leadership over this breed.

The Bouvier needs daily exercise, but should not be jogged with over long distances because of its heavy structure and predisposition to hip problems. Time to train, socialize, exercise, and groom this dog must be made be available.

Briard

Origins: A centuries-old French herder, the Briard was first used to guard herds against wolves and poachers. It was bred with good size and a protective coat.

Appearance: The Briard stands 22 to 27 inches at the shoulder and weighs between 55 and 90 pounds. It has a large, strong, lanky body and a shedding coat that is long and straight or slightly wavy, with a finer undercoat. The head is well coated, with a beard, long, arched, expressive eyebrows, and cropped or uncropped ears. The eyes are almost covered with hair. This breed requires a daily brushing and combing to prevent mats. A shorter clip will lessen the maintenance requirements. The color may be black, gray, or tawny or a combination of two of these colors.

Breed Profile: This lively, independent breed is affectionate with its family and reserved with strangers. Alert and territorial, it may be initially resistant to training. A firm, consistent technique combined with early socialization will be needed to reduce pushy, suspicious behavior. Giving this breed a job such as herding, competition obedience, or agility work will help focus its energy and increase its confidence.

The Briard may chase cars, bikes, and joggers and may not tolerate the hectic activity of young children, perhaps nipping at them in an effort to herd them. Roughhousing and chasing should not be allowed. This breed can also be dog-aggressive.

The Briard may be susceptible to hip dysplasia and eye problems.

Best Home: A house with a fenced yard is essential. The owner of a Briard should be an active, firm leader who desires an athletic, lively, intelligent breed. Daily exercise is mandatory; competition obedience or herding would help focus this breed and build its confidence. Sedentary people should avoid this breed. Spoilers and nervous types may encourage a pushy, nippy, timid attitude. Older children who will not roughhouse or play chase games are okay. The elderly and the disabled may have trouble controlling this active breed. The Briard does better in a dry climate; wet environments tend to cause the coat to become smelly and matted.

Collie

Origins: Developed centuries ago in Scotland, the Collie was first used as a cattle and sheep drover and then as a herder.

Appearance: The Collie stands 23 to 26 inches at the shoulder and weighs between 55 and 75 pounds. It has a large, lithe body and a long muzzle. It comes in two varieties, Rough and Smooth. The Rough (Lassie-type) Collie has a beautiful thick shedding coat with an undercoat, which requires daily brushing. The Smooth Collie's coat is much shorter and requires less care. The color may be sable-and-white, tricolor (black, white, and tan), blue merle (marbled blue-gray, black, and white), or white with sable, tricolor, or blue merle markings.

Breed Profile: The Collie is a large, sensitive, intelligent dog. There are differences in temperament between the two varieties, but let's first discuss what they have in common.

This breed can be noisy. At dog shows we are amazed at how many of the Collies have been debarked, a surgical procedure that we and many veterinarians frown upon. You should not pick a Collie if you live in an apartment or a densely populated area. A Collie should not be left in the yard all day; it will find something to bark at and may bark all day. Without you there to modify this behavior, it will become ingrained and impossible to change. This is a very active dog outside, but it tends to be quite calm indoors.

The Collie tends to be on the sensitive side and does not do well with gruff, overbearing adults or with children tearing around. It needs a calm, predictable environment, and it must be exercised every day. Like the other herding breeds, the Collie tends to chase children, bikes, cars, and joggers if allowed to roam free. Early training is recommended to suppress this instinct.

The Collie responds well to training, provided it is not rushed or overbearing. A well-trained Collie will be tolerant of children.

The Smooth Collie in our experience, can be more aggressive and stubborn than the Rough. Most of the aggressive Collies we have seen have been Smooth. The Smooths also tend to be more energetic than the Roughs.

The Collie is susceptible to hip dysplasia and eye problems. Deafness may occur among the blue merle dogs.

Best Home: A house with a fenced yard is essential. The owner of a Rough Collie should be a patient leader who desires an athletic, sensitive breed. The owner of a Smooth Collie should be slightly firmer and more demanding. Daily exercise is necessary. Herding, obedience, or agility work can help direct this breed's energy and build its confidence. Spoilers and nervous owners may encourage pushy, nippy behavior and will lower the dog's confidence. Overbearing people may provoke fear-biting. Older children are okay provided no rough-housing or chase games are allowed. The elderly and the disabled may have trouble controlling and exercising the Rough Collie and should not consider the Smooth Collie.

German Shepherd

Origins: The German Shepherd is a fairly new breed that
first appeared in Germany only
about one hundred years ago.
Initially used for herding, this
versatile breed has adapted
well to police and military
work, search-and-rescue work,
tracking, bomb detection, and
protection work.

Appearance: The German Shepherd stands 22 to 26 inches at the
shoulder and weighs between 60 and 110 pounds. It has a strong,
muscular body and a medium length, coarse shedding coat with a
softer undercoat, which needs to be brushed daily. The color may
be black, black-and-tan, golden with black-tipped hairs, or gray with
black-tipped hairs. White is strongly discouraged.

Breed Profile: The German Shepherd is a large dog that, though
included in the herding group, is in fact one of the most versatile
breeds. It is strong, agile, loyal, and highly intelligent, and possesses
one of the keenest noses in the dog world. The German Shepherd
is courageous and very territorial and will instinctively protect its
home. It tends to be suspicious of strangers until its owner accepts
the person or persons into their home. The Shepherd becomes
truly bonded to its family, perhaps more so than any other breed,
and consequently can suffer from separation anxiety when apart
from its people. If boarded for a length of time, it can become
depressed, may refuse to eat, and can lose an appreciable amount
of weight.

This breed makes a great family pet when properly trained, and
it will love and protect your children almost to a fault. It can be
suspicious of your children's friends, which could lead to a biting
incident if the child shows fear or flight. The Shepherd may

want to chase cars, bikes, or joggers and may be dog-aggressive.

It is essential to train and socialize a Shepherd from puppyhood with people and other dogs. Training is not always easy with a Shepherd; it is so intelligent that it will think of ways to avoid doing what you are asking of it. The most intelligent breeds, contrary to popular belief, are not the easiest to train. The opposite is often true.

The German Shepherd is extremely perceptive. It is acutely aware of its owner's moods or any change in its environment, however slight. No other breed is so tuned into its world. Socialization must therefore be extensive and must cover as many different situations as possible. Failure to do this may result in an unexpected aggressive or fearful response to certain people or places.

The German Shepherd, because of its great popularity, has been overbred. We see many poor-quality, flighty American-bred Shepherds with behavioral and structural problems. Many suffer from hip dysplasia, shoulder problems, and pan osteitis, an inflammation of the growth plates of the bones, which can be aggravated by keeping a Shepherd puppy on high-protein puppy food past eight months of age, causing too-rapid growth. Breeders who supplement their bloodlines with imported German stock tend to produce more active, stable, structurally sound dogs. *Do not buy a German Shepherd from a pet store.*

Best Home: A house with a secluded fenced yard is essential. The owner of a German Shepherd should be a strong, confident, emotionally secure leader who desires a smart, protective, athletic dog. This is not a breed for an insecure or immature person. The Shepherd is very sensitive and will reflect the mood and emotion of its owner, often with alarming results.

Do not let a Shepherd assert itself against you or achieve dominance in any venue. Like the Rottweiler, it will quickly take charge if you spoil or placate it. Allow this and you open yourself up to aggression problems.

Children are okay provided no roughhousing or chase games are permitted.

Daily exercise is mandatory. Obedience, herding, retrieving, or agility work will direct the Shepherd's energy and build its confidence. The elderly and the disabled may have trouble controlling this active, dominant, intelligent breed. Time to train, exercise, and socialize this dog must be available.

Old English Sheepdog

Origins: Developed in England in the nineteenth century, this breed served as a cattle and sheep drover.

Appearance: The Old English Sheepdog stands 21 to 24 inches at the shoulder and weighs between 60 and 90 pounds. It has a strong, broad body, a large head, a docked tail, and an abundant shaggy, wavy shedding coat with a softer undercoat. This coat, which is the most distinctive feature of the breed, requires daily brushing to prevent mats. It is absorbent and should be kept dry so as to avoid odors. A shorter clip helps reduce maintenance. The color may be gray or blue, often with white markings.

Breed Profile: The Old English is less energetic than other herders. Affectionate with its family, it is suspicious of strangers and can be moody and introspective. It is a stubborn breed and can be passive-resistant, taking a head-in-the-sand attitude when required to obey a command. The training technique should be persistent, precise, and never overbearing; too harsh a trainer could cause timidity and fear-aggression in this breed. Socialization should begin early and will help increase the dog's confidence. Spoiling may lower its confidence and encourage obnoxious, nippy behavior.

The Old English Sheepdog may show dog-aggression and may want to chase cars, bikes, or joggers. It should be okay with older children, but no chase games should be allowed. If left alone for long periods, this dog may bark and become destructive. Though not extremely active, it does need daily exercise.

Best Home: A house with a fenced yard is essential. The owner of an Old English Sheepdog should be a strong, confident, patient leader who desires a somewhat easygoing, serious, discriminating pet that will be initially suspicious of strangers and serve as a good watchdog. Spoiling may encourage pushy, nasty behavior in this breed, and an overbearing owner could incite fear-aggression. Older children who do not roughhouse or chase are okay. The elderly and the disabled might not be able to handle this large breed. Time to train, socialize, exercise, and groom this breed must be available.

Puli

Origins: The Puli is an ancient Hungarian herd-guarding and droving breed whose distinctive corded coat protects it against inclement weather and also against the bites of wolves. Its medium size allowed it to traverse rocky terrain more easily than the larger herders.

Appearance: The Puli stands 15 to 18 inches at the shoulder and weighs between 28 and 35 pounds. It has a strong, medium-size body and a long, thick, weatherproof, shedding coat that forms cords as the undercoat and outer coat blend together. These cords cover the entire body, including the eyes. It is hard to keep this high maintenance style from becoming malodorous and mildewed. The coat is easier to maintain if kept combed out and clipped short. The color may be black, gray, or white.

Breed Profile: An active, independent, willful breed, the Puli can often be a moody, suspicious animal. Loyal to only one or two people, it is very suspicious of strangers and is capable of biting if threatened or annoyed. It is an excellent watchdog that can be clever but extremely stubborn. Training should be firm and persistent. The most difficult command to teach it may be the Come. If spoiled, this breed will become controlling and nasty. Socialization from puppyhood is essential to reduce its aversion to strangers.

The Puli can be dog-aggressive and has a high prey drive toward small animals. It is not recommended for families with children. It may want to chase cars, bikes, and joggers and is likely to bite trespassers.

The Puli barks and can be destructive if left alone for too long. It needs regular exercise and may enjoy herding or agility work.

This breed can be susceptible to hip dysplasia and ear infections. It may develop skin fungi if the coat is allowed to mildew.

Best Home: A house with a yard is preferable. The owner of a Puli should be a strong, competent leader who has experience dealing with dominant, potentially aggressive dogs and who desires a smart, alert, loyal breed that will watch the house and property. Nervous people and spoilers may encourage pushy, aggressive behavior in this breed. We do not recommend this breed for families with children. The elderly and the disabled may not be able to establish dominance with a Puli. Time to train, socialize, exercise, and groom this breed must be available.

Shetland Sheepdog

Origins: Developed in the Shetland Islands of Scotland in the late eighteenth century, this breed was used for herding and guarding. Its small size was well suited to the rocky terrain of the islands.

Appearance: The Shetland Sheepdog, or Sheltie stands 13 to 16 inches at the shoulder and weighs between 14 and 25 pounds. Shelties look like miniature rough Collies. Some are bred to be quite petite, and others are bred much larger. It has a trim, sturdy body and an almost foxlike face. Its shedding coat is medium-long, straight, and hard, with a softer undercoat. The hair does not lie flat, but rather stands up and away from the body. A daily brushing is needed to prevent matting. The color may be sable, black, black-and-tan, or blue merle (mottled blue, gray, black, tan and white).

Breed Profile: A lively, intelligent, inquisitive breed, the Sheltie is normally affectionate with its owners and suspicious of strangers. It can be a sensitive dog and may show timidity in unfamiliar situations. Training should begin early and should be patient and precise. If trained properly, the Sheltie can be a top-notch obedience dog. If spoiled, it may become very controlling and nippy and will lack confidence. Handling and socialization are important and should begin in puppyhood.

The Sheltie may chase cars, bikes, and joggers and will bark loudly. Though normally good with children, it will not tolerate roughhousing. Chase games should also be forbidden.

We have found that the larger Shelties tend to be calmer and less timid than the more petite specimens.

The Sheltie is susceptible to eye problems, and deafness may be a problem in the blue merles.

Best Home: An apartment is adequate if the dog is exercised. Remember, however, that Shelties bark a lot. The owner of a Sheltie should be a patient, consistent leader who desires a smart, busy companion that can excel at competition obedience and in agility work. This is not a quiet, easygoing breed. Spoilers and nervous owners may encourage bossy, nippy behavior and will lower the dog's confidence. Older children who do not roughhouse or chase are okay. The elderly and the disabled can own this breed if they are able to train and exercise it. Time for training, socialization, exercise, and grooming must be available.

Welsh Corgi, Cardigan and Pembroke

Origins: First developed in Wales, Corgis were used as cattle drovers. They could also clear a herder's land of a neighboring herder's marauding cattle. These smart, bold dogs, though low to the ground, have the body and temperament of a larger dog.

Appearance: Corgis come in two varieties, the Cardigan and the Pembroke. The Cardigan Welsh Corgi stands 10.5 to 12.5 inches at the shoulder and weighs between 30 and 40 pounds. It has a sturdy body and short legs. The shedding coat is short, smooth, and easy to maintain. The Pembroke Welsh Corgi tends to be smaller than the Cardigan,

standing 10 to 12 inches at the shoulder and weighing between 25 and 30 pounds. Its head is smaller, the ears are pointed instead of rounded, and the tail is docked very short. The shedding coat is of a finer texture and is also easy to care for. The Cardigan may be brindle, black, brown, red, or blue merle (mottled blue, black, and gray), all with white markings. The color of the Pembroke may be red, sable, fawn, black, or tan, all with white markings.

Breed Profile: Both Corgis are intelligent, sharp, strong-willed dogs that show great affection and loyalty to their owners. Both have a sassy side and can resist obedience training, particularly the Down or the Come command. The Cardigan has a bold, dominant nature and must be trained from puppyhood to combat its stubborn streak. Without frequent socialization, it can become wary of persons outside the family, and it may sometimes be snappy, particularly when surprised during a nap. It is a good watchdog with a big-dog bark.

Temperamentally the Pembroke is very similar to the Cardigan, though perhaps more sensitive and possibly more cautious with children and strangers.

Both breeds make good family pets if training and socialization are begun early. They can live well in an apartment, but they are quite athletic and need regular exercise.

Corgis can make good obedience dogs and will be happier if they continue learning. They are working dogs that need a job to do in order to feel confident. Never let a Corgi run free in the neighborhood, as this will only encourage the dog to chase cars, bikes, children, and joggers. It may also make the dog suspicious of strangers and will encourage biting—something you certainly want to avoid.

Corgis can be susceptible to eye problems and structural problems.

Best Home: An apartment is adequate if the dog is exercised daily. Keep in mind, however, that both breeds have a big-dog bark. The owner of a Pembroke or Cardigan Welsh Corgi should be an active, confident leader who desires a busy, intelligent breed that is loyal and playful. Spoiling may encourage pushy, nippy behavior. Older children are okay if no roughhousing or chasing is permitted.

Corgis love to retrieve a ball or a Frisbee, and this type of constructive exercise is just what they need. The elderly and the disabled can own either breed if they can train and exercise them. Time to train, socialize, and exercise the dog must be available.

The Miscellaneous Group

The dogs in this class have not yet been recognized for registration with the AKC. This is a probationary class; dogs listed here often go on to be registered and placed in one of the seven groups. The following breeds are currently listed in the Miscellaneous Class:

American Eskimo Dog
Australian Kelpie
Border Collie
Cavalier King Charles Spaniel
Greater Swiss Mountain Dog
Spinoni Italiani

In addition to these breeds, we will describe the Jack Russell Terrier and the Pit Bull Terrier, and we will discuss wolf hybrids, which unfortunately have increased in popularity in the past few years. We will provide more information about the most popular dogs in this class than about the rare breeds.

American Eskimo Dog

Origins: The ancestry of the American Eskimo Dog can be traced back to the spitz-type dogs of Germany and northern Europe.

Appearance: The American Eskimo Dog may be any one of three sizes: the Standard stands 15 to 18 inches at the shoulder and weighs between 25 and 35 pounds; the Miniature stands 12 to 15 inches and weigh between 12 and 20 pounds; the Toy stands under 12 inches and weighs between 6 and 10 pounds.

Breed Profile: This breed is independent and energetic and has a great deal of nervous energy. Though affectionate with its owners, the American Eskimo can be initially reserved with strangers. This intelligent breed can excel in obedience if trained from puppy-hood. The Eskimo can be a barker and may be stubborn. It can do well in an apartment if exercised daily. The owner of this breed should desire a playful, impetuous pet. Older children are okay provided they do not tease or roughhouse. A spoiled Eskimo can become nippy and timid around strangers. We have known several Eskis that were quite aggresive as a result of being spoiled.

Australian Kelpie

This herding breed is rare in the United States. It stands 20 to 23 inches at the shoulder and weighs between 45 and 55 pounds. It has a short- to medium-length shedding coat. The Kelpie is a strong, active herder with a temperament similar to that of the Australian Cattle Dog. It needs lots of space and requires strong leadership. It is not the best choice for a family pet.

Border Collie

Origins: Developed in England and Scotland during the nineteenth century, the Border Collie was a result of mixing the bloodlines of several working collies of that time. A phenomenal herder, the Border Collies will literally walk across the backs of the sheep in its herd in order to most quickly cross to the other side. It can control the sheep with its fixed stare, a Border Collie trademark.

Appearance: The Border Collie stands 17 to 21 inches at the shoulder and weighs between 38 and 52 pounds. It has a medium-length shedding coat that requires regular brushing. The color may be black-and-white, gray-and-white, or blue merle (blue, black, and gray).

Breed Profile: Arguably the most intelligent breed, the Border Collie is an active, alert dog that, though affectionate with its owners, may be very timid and reserved around strangers. It is a fascinating breed, capable of excelling at obedience and agility work.

The Border Collie can become fixated on a certain toy or activity. It will fetch until it drops.

This breed's level of intelligence can create a stubborn mind-set; patience and consistency are necessary in order to train this sensitive breed. We do not recommend this breed for families with children, as it may snap if irritated or teased.

Exercise this breed often, but do not let it off the leash unless it has learned the Come command perfectly. If allowed to run loose, the Border Collie may chase cars, bikes, or joggers and may attempt to herd children by nipping at their heels.

The Border Collie can be susceptible to hip dysplasia, eye problems, and, particularly the blue merle variety, hearing problems.

Best Home: A house with a well-fenced yard is essential. The owner of a Border Collie should be a firm, patient leader who desires an extremely intelligent breed capable of excelling in obedience, herding, or agility work. This breed is not recommended for those who have children. Daily exercise is essential; the Border Collie lives to fetch a ball or a Frisbee. Socialization beginning in puppyhood will help minimize this breed's timidity around strangers. The elderly and the disabled may have trouble controlling this active breed.

Cavalier King Charles Spaniel

Origins: Developed in England, this breed is considered a companion dog.

Appearance: The Cavalier King Charles Spaniel stands 11 to 12 inches at the shoulder and weighs between 12 and 18 pounds. It has a long, fine, straight, shedding coat that requires a daily brushing. The color may be black-and-tan, tricolor (white, black, and red), Ruby (red), or Blenheim (white and red).

Breed Profile: This breed is gentle, affectionate, and sweet-tempered. It takes very quickly to strangers and should be fine with children, provided no roughhousing is permitted. The training technique should be gentle and precise. Though easily spoiled, this breed normally does not become nippy. It makes a great companion dog for the elderly or disabled.

Greater Swiss Mountain Dog

Originally a cart-pulling dog, the Greater Swiss Mountain Dog stands 25 to 28 inches at the shoulder and may weigh 125 to 130 pounds. Its shedding coat is short. The temperament of this breed is very similar to that of the Bernese Mountain Dog, albeit without the phobic tendency. It is rarely seen in the United States.

Spinoni Italiani

The Spinoni Italiani is an Italian pointing griffon, slightly larger in size but similar in temperament to the Petit Basset Griffon Vendéen. It has an excellent sense of smell. This breed is rarely seen in the United States.

Jack Russell Terrier

Origins: Developed in England to work with foxhounds, the Jack Russell Terrier has excelled at hunting field trials and as a ratter.

Appearance: The Jack Russell Terrier stands 11 to 14 inches at the shoulder and weighs between 10 and 16 pounds. It has a sturdy, compact body and either a short, hard coat or a rough, wiry coat. Both coat types shed but are easy to maintain. The color is normally white with patches of black and tan.

Breed Profile: This stubborn, energetic little dog is personable and inquisitive. Though the Jack Russell is an intelligent breed, it can be difficult to train because of its high activity level and its obstinate, driven nature. Affectionate with its family and normally friendly to strangers, the Jack Russell is easily distracted, particularly by scent. This breed needs regular activity to curb its restlessness. It loves to play with a ball and can be taught to retrieve quite well. If left alone for too long, it may become noisy and destructive.

The training technique should be firm and consistent from puppyhood on. Spoiling may encourage nippy, bossy behavior. The Jack Russell can be very mouthy; this tendency should be curbed right from the start. Most Jack Russells cannot be trusted off the leash, and this breed may show a high prey drive toward small animals.

Best Home: A house with a fenced yard is preferable, but not necessary, for this little dynamo. The owner of a Jack Russell Terrier should desire an active, inquisitive dog that, if trained properly, can excel at obedience or agility work. This is not the breed for an easygoing owner. Children should be okay, provided no roughhousing is permitted, but watch for mouthy behavior on the part of the dog, a sign of disrespect. The elderly and the disabled might have trouble controlling this active breed.

Pit Bull Terrier

Origins: The Pit Bull Terrier has the same general history as the American Staffordshire Terrier and the Staffordshire Bull Terrier. It is considered a different breed, however, and has suffered a worse reputation than its two cousins. The breeding of this dog has been historically inconsistent; temperament has varied greatly because of this.

Appearance: The Pit Bull Terrier stands 17 to 20 inches at the shoulder and weighs between 55 and 80 pounds. It has a muscular, athletic body and a short, shedding, low-maintenance coat. Colors include black, brindle, fawn, and patched.

Breed Profile: The ideal Pit Bull Terrier is similar in temperament to the American Staffordshire Terrier, but is perhaps a bit more energetic and confident. It is very loving with its family and, if properly socialized, can be very affectionate with friends of the family. A powerful dog, the Pit Bull needs firm but not overbearing leadership from puppyhood on, as well as lots of socialization. This breed can be extremely dog-aggressive and should not be let off the leash except in fenced areas. An owner or trainer should never use harsh methods on this sensitive breed.

The problems with this breed have resulted from the haphazard, careless backyard breeding that continues to go on, combined with the desire by some macho types to create an antisocial biting machine. These individuals often create dogs that are a menace to the community and to other animals. A poorly bred and socialized Pit Bull is a loaded weapon. This breed has tremendous drive and biting strength and, once instigated, will not stop its attack. The breeding of this dog needs to be more carefully monitored by responsible, concerned breeders. Many breed clubs nationwide are now attempting to do just that.

Best Home: A house with a secluded fenced yard is essential. The owner of a Pit Bull Terrier should be a firm, physically capable leader who desires an affectionate, powerful, active breed. Training and socialization should begin in puppyhood and continue throughout the dog's life. This breed is not recommended for those who have young children. Also, it is safer to own a Pit Bull singly, with no other dogs or small animals in the house. The elderly and the disabled should not own this breed. Pick a Pit Bull breeder with the *utmost care!*

Wolf Hybrids

A wolf hybrid is produced by breeding dogs with animals that are partially or totally wolf. Many of these animals are half or three-quarters German Shepherd or Malamute and half or one-quarter timber wolf. Any percentage of wolf blood in an animal, however, will classify it as a hybrid. Over the years we have had a num-

ber of wolf hybrids come to us for training and behavior modification. Most of them do not make good pets, and some are downright dangerous.

A wolf is not a dog. *It is a wolf.* Wolves do not act like domesticated dogs. They are smarter, much flightier, and highly unpredictable. They are not by nature aggressive toward human beings, but they can be deadly when provoked. Wolves are extremely sensitive and independent and do not respond well to obedience training. They are wild animals and should remain so. They do not make good guards. In fact, they run from confrontation unless there is no alternative.

When a wolf is crossed with a domestic dog—say, a German Shepherd—the resulting hybrids can have very unpredictable temperaments. The flightiness of the wolf can combine with the more gregarious nature of the Shepherd to produce an overtly dangerous animal.

Hybrids tend to panic if trained with the same methods used on dogs. They are not at all trustworthy with children and will have an extremely high prey drive toward small animals. They will be restless and destructive, particularly if left alone. Their strong pack instinct requires them to be part of a group; separation can cause panic that could result in escape and disaster.

In addition, many hybrids will not respond to the vaccines used on the domesticated dog. The rabies vaccine in particular does not seem to work properly on hybrids that have fifty percent or more wolf blood.

Do not get a wolf hybrid.

Is There a Mutt in Your Life?

Any dog with two or more ancestors of differing breeds is a mixed-breed dog. There are probably as many mixed-breed dogs in this country as there are purebreds, largely the result of failure to alter or contain pets properly. It is important to realize, of course, that each of today's purebred dogs began as a calculated experiment in selective breeding by a fancier with a definite purpose in mind—to engineer a new breed to suit a specific need. The Weimaraner, for example, came about as a result of various crosses between the Bloodhound and several pointer types including the German Short-haired Pointer. The intent was to create a dog with superior scenting ability, speed, strength, courage, and drive, something that did not exist at that time. Weimaraners were used to track and contain big game, including wolves and bears, something that Pointers and Bloodhounds weren't fully capable of doing. In effect, the Weimaraner and almost all other purebred dogs started out as mixed breeds. It is therefore important not to snobbishly feel that your purebred Golden Retriever is superior to a mixed-breed dog simply on the basis of its consistent, carefully monitored lineage.

Mixed-breed dogs are normally no better or worse than purebred dogs with regard to temperament and physiology. It must be remembered that a mixed-breed dog is simply the product of pure-bred animals. There is no process occuring that would make mixed-breed dogs far better or far worse than purebreds. Some people insist that mixed breeds are hardier than purebreds because they come from a larger gene pool, but this is not generally true (though in some instances, when too small a group of purebred dogs has been inbred, physiological and behavioral abnormalities can occur). If today's mixed breeds were farther removed from their purebred ancestors—say, ten or twenty generations—there might be validity to that claim. But this is not the case. The vast majority of mixed breeds had a purebred parent or grandparent and will therefore approximate their physiology and temperament, albeit with some minor and often interesting variations.

Mixed-breed dogs are always available, unlike purebreds, which often require a search and then a waiting period. Shelters in this country are filled with mixed breeds of all ages, as a result of the irresponsibility of owners. This brings up an ethical dilemma: do you shop for a purebred or save a mixed breed from imminent euthanasia? This is a tough call. Mixed breeds are very affordable, usually costing only the price of altering, licensing, and vaccinations. Purebred dogs on the other hand can cost anywhere from two hundred dollars for a pet-quality pup of a popular breed to well over a thousand dollars for a large or rare show-quality dog. In addition, if you get a mixed breed through a shelter, you will most likely be provided with some educational material, and you may also be given an opportunity to enroll in an obedience class.

There are drawbacks to acquiring a mixed breed dog, however. It is hard to predict the size that a mixed breed pup will attain when fully grown. In a year you could end up with a two-hundred-pound drooling monster. Even more important, you will usually know little or nothing about the dog's history or breeding. Was the dog abused? Hit by a car? What were its parent and littermates like? You will have no way of predicting the temperament of a mixed breed pup if you don't observe the parents and the litter. A private owner might have the parents and litter, but shelters usually don't have either available. You may not be able to talk to the previous owners, who may be unknown, unwilling to talk, or less than honest about any problems that existed or still exist. One great benefit of buying a purebred dog is being able to see the parents and to gauge the pup's temperament by studying the rest of the litter. Are the parents friendly, aggressive, neurotic, confident, or phobic? Is the pup more or less dominant than its littermates? All of this information is usually unavailable to those acquiring a mixed breed.

It is harder to predict the breed-specific behavior of a mixed-breed dog. We can tell you with some certainty that a Beagle will be noisy, that a Rottweiler will be pushy, and that a Saluki will be reserved with strangers. That can't be done as easily with a mixed-breed dog. The only way to attempt it is to first identify what breed each parent was, either from firsthand knowledge or by observing the dog itself and trying to make an educated guess as to what breeds appear to be present. First look at any book containing color photos of the breeds. Then look at the color, length, and texture of the mixed breed dog's coat. Look at its leg and back length, its bite, its ears and tail. Pay attention also to its behavior. Is it sniffy like a scent hound? Does it want to herd like a Shepherd or Collie? Is it a natural retriever like a Lab? Does it have a high prey drive like a terrier? Its behavior in combination with its appearance could help you determine what sort of dog you have. This is not an exact science of course, but it can be an interesting exercise.

Certain breed crosses should absolutely be avoided. For example, a Rottweiler-Chow mix might be adorable, but it would probably be a dominant, aggressive, stubborn handful. A mixture of Chinese Shar-Pei and Pointer would certainly be a hyperactive, aggressive, unpredictable mess. Some crosses might be acceptable, however. The reserved nature of a Greyhound might be ameliorated by the gregarious, playful attitude of a Lab, for example, and the quiet, dignified temperament of the Greyhound might have a quieting effect on the energetic Lab temperament.

Recommendations

We recommend that, if you opt for a mixed breed, you consider a four- to six-month-old dog. By the time a dog is four months old, its personality and temperament are basically established. For example, if a five-month-old dog is very shy, it may be shy the rest of its life. This shyness can be modified through confidence-building and socialization, but the basic temperament won't change.

Puppies are adorable, but unless you can observe the behavior of the parents and littermates, you will have no way of predicting your dog's temperament, personality, and ultimate size. A four- to six-month-old dog, however, will show its true colors and yet be young enough to learn quickly and well. It is also possible (though not assured) that a dog of this age might be housebroken to some extent. You will also be more able to observe any medical or structural problems, which wouldn't be as evident in a young pup.

Another option is to get an older mixed-breed dog—the shelters are filled with them. Again, the personalities of these dogs are usually well defined. They are often housebroken, and many have had some obedience training, which will make them easier to deal with.

You must be aware, however, that an older dog may have been abandoned because it has medical problems or because it became aggressive after a profound change occurred in its environment. Often the addition of a baby, a puppy, or a new spouse can set off an older dog, and you must understand that major behavioral problems will be more difficult to modify in an older dog than in a younger animal.

Where to Find a Good Mixed-Breed Dog

The first place to look is a qualified, reputable shelter such as the Humane Society or a county-supported facility. These are normally adequately staffed and funded, and many of them provide plenty of information as well as basic obedience classes. The adoptable dogs will be altered, often free of charge and, if old enough, will be fully inoculated. There are also many privately run nonprofit shelters throughout the country (ask a veterinarian or look in the Yellow Pages) that do an admirable job, though they are not always funded as well as a county facility. These normally charge a nominal fee for altering and inoculations. Many also offer obedience classes for a small fee.

For-profit shelters are also a source for mixed-breed dogs, but the profit motive must always be taken into consideration. You may not get the straight scoop on a dog, or the health of the dogs might be suspect because of overcrowding.

Many look to newspapers to find dogs. Doing this is similar to buying a car from a private advertisement. Have the sellers represented their product honestly? Has it been well maintained? What are the owners like? Why are they selling this dog or giving it away? Their motivation for giving up the dog must always be suspect. Is the dog aggressive or destructive? Does it bark incessantly? Is it housebroken? Is it their dog or just a stray that they are selling for a quick buck? Be observant and skeptical when you read a newspaper ad. Watch the dog's interaction with the people, and observe the environment. Is it clean and well maintained? Are the people forthright about why they are unwilling to keep the dog? It is your job to find that out.

Some pet shops also sell mixed-breed dogs, which are often a result of the accidental breeding of two purebred puppy-mill dogs. Though we know of some respectable pet shops, as a general rule we frown on getting any dog this way. These stores have a reputation for providing low-quality, poorly bred dogs. Pet shop dogs also often lack proper dog-to-dog social skills and usually have terrible house-trainings habits due to being in cages constantly. They never learn to differentiate between the right and wrong place to go; they just go on paper in their cage. These dogs are very hard to housebreak, especially if they have been in the pet shop for a long time.

The case of the stray dog is a heartbreaking one. Many of us have befriended a stray, or at least provided one with food or water. We know of many that, after being brought back to health and trained, have become superb pets. The problem with strays is that you have no idea what you are getting. There is no shelter acting as a middleman or filtering agent. Is the dog diseased, dysplastic, arthritic, infectious? Does it have severe behavioral problems? We advise you to avoid adopting a stray unless it is temporary, in lieu of locating the real owners.

In conclusion, a mix can be just as smart, healthy, and rewarding as a purebred. It is just a bit harder to discern the good from the bad due to limited knowledge of the dog's heritage and history.

Choosing the Right Dog from Within a Breed

Choosing the breed of dog that best suits your situation is only the first important step. Equally important is choosing the right dog from within that breed. The automobile analogy is again useful: your decision to purchase the most suitable new vehicle for your needs may be a good one, but it will mean little if the dealer you buy from has inferior stock, an inept service department, or unethical standards.

In searching for the breed you desire, we strongly advise you to avoid pet shops. They often sell inferior animals that are mass-produced at huge puppy mills whose bottom line is volume, not quality. Pet shops that sell dogs prey on the vulnerability of impulse buyers who cannot resist the cute little puppy cavorting in the window. Many of these dogs are physiologically or behaviorally flawed. Some have medical problems that can be hard or impossible to cure. You will probably not see a pet shop puppy's parents; they are too busy being repeatedly bred at the puppy mill. (We know of puppy mill brood bitches that are bred repeatedly from their first heat, at seven to nine months, until they are seven or eight years of age, when they become exhausted and are of no further use to the business. These bitches are then routinely destroyed.) Chances are that the pet shop puppy was much too young when separated from its littermates. A puppy that is not allowed to socialize with its littermates during the first five to seven weeks of life can become antisocial and dog-aggressive. Additionally, these puppies often spend three to four months at the pet shop waiting for a buyer. During this time virtually no housebreaking is attempted, which means the animal will be difficult to housebreak once it goes to a home. It has not been taught to distinguish between clean and dirty conditions and often spends much of its time on soiled straw or newspaper.

Private parties often offer puppies and older dogs for sale through the classified advertisements. They may be sincere, but they often have little or no breeding experience and are usually selling puppies produced through an accidental breeding. The parent dogs may be of questionable lineage, and the care of the puppies by first-time breeders may not have been adequate. Though many fine dogs have been produced and sold by private sellers, we feel that this is a risky way to buy a dog. Breeding sound puppies takes experience and should be left to the professionals.

Animal shelters always have purebred and mixed-breed dogs up for adoption. Purebred puppies are less common at shelters than are dogs in the six- to twelve-month range, usually the age at which behavioral problems first begin to appear, causing many frustrated owners to give up and take the animal into a shelter. Many of these dogs, with structure and leadership, could become fine pets. However, the dog's history may be unavailable to you, making the choice a risky one. The dog may have behavioral problems that could be difficult to modify.

An experienced, caring breeder with a history of producing sound dogs is the best source of a purebred puppy. Professional breeders are the most important players in the evolution and character of a breed. Whether a breeder focuses more on conformation (appearance) or temperament can affect a breed's popularity and reputation for years to come, and these breeders have learned from their mistakes. Breeding is a beloved hobby for most of them. It is rarely a profitable venture.

Finding a Good Breeder

Ask veterinarians, qualified obedience instructors, groomers, or the managers of reputable shelters to recommend a breeder. Most of them have contact with dogs produced by quality breeders, and they will know where you can find a healthy dog with an amiable temperament. If you know someone who owns a great dog of the breed you desire, then ask him or her for the breeder's name.

National breed clubs can put you in touch with breeders all over the country, including some in your area. Breeders who belong to national breed clubs are likely to be ethical and successful at what they do.

Attending dog shows is another way to meet breeders. It will also afford you the opportunity to see their show dogs in person.

Many reputable breeders run ads in dog magazines, though many of them will not be located close enough to you to make a trip there feasible, something we highly recommend.

Choosing a Breeder

Once you have located several breeders who produce the breed you desire, we recommend that you visit all of them before deciding on a puppy. Compare their facilities, and beware of the hard sell. Do not be pressured into buying a puppy because the breeder says there are three other prospective buyers on their way over. Also, do not buy a puppy simply because the breeder isn't planning to produce another litter any time soon.

Pay attention to first impressions. Which of the breeders is open, informative, and friendly? Which are closed-mouthed and cautious? A good breeder will be honest and will want to place the puppy in the best home possible. Breeders should also want to know about you. Are you responsible enough to own a dog? Do you have a house with a fenced yard, or do you live in a studio apartment? Do you own other pets? A good breeder will want to ensure the welfare of his or her dog, for the animal's sake and for the future success of the breed.

Observe the general appearance of the facility. Is it clean and well maintained? Do the animals appear to be healthy? Is the breeder's home neat and orderly or messy and chaotic? You wouldn't buy groceries in a filthy store infested with vermin, so why tolerate these conditions when shopping for a dog?

Check the area where the puppies are housed. It should be clean, warm, and comfortable. Water, bedding, and perhaps a few chew toys should be available. If this area is littered with excrement, the puppies may have become used to these conditions and may not understand that the sleeping area is not also a place to eliminate. Housebreaking these puppies could be difficult.

The friendliest dogs are usually those that have been handled by humans from the time they were only a few days old. Successful breeders understand this and will have regular handling sessions with the puppies every day. Many bring the puppies into their home each day to acclimate them to this environment. Avoid those breeders who keep their puppies isolated from people.

No breeder should allow a puppy to leave the litter before it is seven weeks of age. Proper socialization within the litter is ensured during this important period. Puppies that leave too soon often become dog-aggressive and antisocial. Breeders who are willing to let their puppies go too early are not doing their job properly. Avoid them.

Proper record-keeping is an essential part of the breeding process. Breeders should have the pedigrees of all of their available dogs and should provide you with the accurate date of birth as well as all vaccination records. The breeder must also give you a blue AKC registration application for your puppy. You will fill this out and mail it to the American Kennel Club; the AKC will then send you your puppy's registration certificate. A sales contract should be provided as well. Read this document carefully; some contracts specify co-ownership between you and the breeder, and some require you to alter the pet within a certain period.

The breeder should allow you to see the parents of the available litter and should provide you with copies of their pedigrees and health records, including their vaccination records and OFA certificates, which indicate the status of the parents' hips. The appearance and behavior of the parents is a good indicator of the breeder's abilities. Often the breeder has only one parent on premises, usually the bitch. Many use the services of another breeder's stud dog to mate with their bitch. If this is the case, you may only get to observe one parent. Feel free to request information on the missing parent. If the breeder balks at this, move on.

Above all, take your time. Choosing the right dog for you is an important decision. Do not give in to sales pressure or to the first chubby puppy you see. Comparison shopping works for all purchases, including dogs. Visit several breeders before deciding!

Selecting a Puppy

Once you have chosen a breeder, it is time to pick out the puppy from the available litter. A good rule of thumb is to avoid extremes. Disqualify from contention any puppies that are excessively submissive or fearful, and avoid puppies that are extremely dominant or bullying. Fierce food or toy guarding, exaggerated barking or biting, submissive urination, and extreme apathy are all bad signs in young puppies. Curiosity, however, is good, as are playfulness and confidence. Above all, do not let the puppy pick you. The big fat one that charges at you and monopolizes your attention may win your heart, but it is very likely the most dominant, and it will be a handful.

Decide which sex puppy you prefer. Males tend to be larger and more dominant, curious, and courageous. They are better workers and are not as moody. They do not come into season and are cheaper to alter. They are also more likely to fight and roam. Females are normally smaller, less dominant and defiant, and more sensitive and moody. They normally come into heat twice a year, but they are less likely to fight and to roam. If you have chosen an extremely dominant breed such as the Rottweiler or Chow Chow, you would be wise to consider a female. A male might be better if you have decided on a less dominant breed such as a Maltese or a Soft-Coated Wheaten Terrier.

Do not choose two puppies from the same litter. Littermates bond very closely to each other, making it much more difficult for the owner to establish leadership. If you want two dogs, properly raise one puppy first, and then consider another, perhaps two or three years later. The older dog will serve as a role model for the puppy, making your job that much easier.

Observe the litter without interacting with it. How do the puppies look? Are there some large puppies and one or two runts? Do you see any glaring structural problems in any of them? Is there any loose stool or vomit present? Are some puppies very lethargic? If the breeder has classified some of the litter as show quality and the rest as pet quality, ask why. Also inquire as to the number of males and females. If there are only one or two puppies of the gender you desire, you will not have as much of a range of temperaments to choose from. Avoid picking a puppy that is the sole survivor in the litter; it will have missed the early crucial social interaction that goes on in a normal litter.

Next, enter the kennel and interact with the litter. How do they react to your presence? Do some run away and hide, bark and charge, or show playful curiosity? This last reaction is the most desirable. Next, examine each one and look for any overt physical problems. Look for eye or nose discharge, bloodshot eyes, mange, overly dry skin or coat, and fleas. Is the puppy's belly bloated? This might indicate worms, a condition that most puppies have and must be treated for. Look in their mouths to make sure that the gums are a healthy pink and not whitish gray. During this procedure, take note of how the puppies react to being handled. Do they fight and bite? Struggle and then submit? Show great fear?

Next, interact separately with each puppy. Here are four tests you should perform with each puppy in order to determine whether it is normal, dominant, or submissive:

Tests

1. Hold each puppy up so that its feet are a few inches off the floor. Observe its reaction:

A *normal* puppy will struggle for a few seconds and then settle down. This reaction indicates spirit but also a willingness to accept authority.

A *dominant* puppy will continue struggling and may howl and bite.

A *submissive* puppy will just dangle passively and accept the situation or, in severe cases, panic and submissively urinate.

2. Hold each puppy on its back in your lap. Comfort it by stroking its belly and talking to it softly. Observe its reaction:

A *normal* puppy will struggle briefly, then settle. This is the response that most buyers should look for.

A *dominant* puppy will struggle constantly, howl, and perhaps try to bite.

A *submissive* puppy will succumb and perhaps urinate or, in an extreme case, panic.

3. Set the puppy on its feet on the floor. Then toss a ball or a crumpled piece of paper away from the puppy and observe its reaction:

A *normal* puppy will chase the object, play with it, and perhaps bring it back to you if you call out to it. It will allow you to take the object away without much fuss.

A *dominant* puppy will chase the object, take it to a corner, and ignore you when you call out to it. It may growl at you if you attempt to reclaim the object.

A *submissive* puppy may not react at all to the object or may actually be afraid of it.

4. Crouch down a few feet from the puppy and encourage it to come to you by clapping or whistling. Observe its reaction:

A *normal* puppy will happily come over to you in a confident, playful manner.

A *dominant* puppy will either charge you and jump up on you recklessly or completely ignore you.

A *submissive* puppy may hide in a corner or come over cautiously and expose its belly, perhaps even urinating upon being touched.

Let us consider extremely submissive behavior to be far left of center, normal to be at the center, and extremely dominant to be far right of center. Most buyers who are looking for a loving, trainable family pet should consider a puppy that performs as close to the center as possible. If you desire a working or obedience dog, or if you are a robust, physically imposing person, you may wish to consider a puppy that is slightly to the right of center. If you are a quiet, slight person, look for a puppy that is slightly left of center.

When dealing with a dominant breed such as the Rottweiler, Mastiff, or German Shepherd, you would do well to consider a puppy that is slightly left of center. When dealing with a submissive breed such as the Maltese, Greyhound, or Wheaten Terrier, you might wish to consider a puppy that is slightly right of center. In all cases, *avoid the extremes.*

The two tests that follow should also be performed. Neither will help you establish whether the puppy is normal, dominant or submissive, but both will aid you in determining how sociable the puppy is with people, and how confident it is when faced with an unknown.

Testing Sociability with People:

Put a few toys down in the room. Quickly walk away from the puppy and observe its reaction:

A favorable response would be the puppy running happily after you, regardless of what else might be occurring. This shows that the puppy in question highly desires the company of people—a trait that is advantageous. This puppy should be easy to train, and should learn to focus well on you instead of distractions.

An unfavorable response would have the puppy ignoring you and investigating something else, perhaps a toy on the floor or a sound coming from another room. This puppy may not value interaction with humans over its own desire to investigate its surroundings. It may not be as easy to train as the puppy that values human interaction above all else. A puppy that ignores you in this way may have an unfocused or independent mindset that could be a prelude to dominant behavior.

Testing Confidence:

Do not perform this test if the puppy is from eight to eleven weeks of age, as this is the "fear imprint stage." During this period, sudden noises or unexpected, scary events can have a profound, lasting effect on the puppy.

Wait until the puppy is not paying attention to you. Then, without the puppy seeing you, throw some item down on the floor. It should be something that will make a fairly loud, sudden noise, perhaps a steel pan or container of some sort. Do not throw it down too close to the puppy. Observe its reaction:

A favorable response would have the puppy showing some caution at first, but quickly recovering and perhaps showing some curiosity toward the object. This puppy is confident and well-adjusted, and does not show irrational fear.

An unfavorable reaction would have the puppy howling and bolting in fear, heading for the farthest corner of the room, perhaps even urinating or defecating. This puppy lacks confidence, and could end up being fearful of unexpected situations or persons. Avoid a puppy that reacts in this way, as it might become fear-aggressive.

Choosing the right dog for your lifestyle is crucial to successful pet ownership. There are five key steps to successful ownership:

Self-Appraisal: Know your personality, body type, and potential for leadership. Are you large or small, active or sedentary, extroverted or introverted, nurturing or distant, loud or soft? Be honest with yourself. Are you responsible enough to own a dog? If so, are you the type of owner who will be best for the breed that interests you? If not, choose a breed that more closely suits you.

Choice of a Breed: Go through the breed profiles carefully and choose several breeds that most closely suit your personality and environment. Do not settle on just one; there will be several breeds that suit your situation. Then make a point of seeing each of these breeds before you choose one.

Choice of a Dog: Follow the steps outlined at the beginning of this chapter. Take your time, and do not fall for the first puppy you see! Make sure you are totally comfortable with the breeder before you make a decision.

Training: Enroll your dog in a basic obedience class as soon as you can, whether it is a puppy or an adult dog. A class will be available in your area, either through the Humane Society or through a private business. What you learn will be invaluable and may be the key to happy, successful ownership. If you do not feel comfortable with the style of teaching, however, then feel free to leave and find another class that is more to your liking. Trust your instincts, as there are some bad instructors out there who might do more harm than good to your dog.

Commitment and Consistency: Dogs are not cats. They require daily attention and training. You must provide your dog with consistent leadership, guidance, and stimulation. Without these things both you and your dog will be unhappy. With them you will learn to appreciate each other. And that's what having a dog is all about.